# B.R.A.N.D.
# Before Your Resumé

## Your Marketing Guide for Veterans & Military Service Members Entering Civilian Life

Graciela Tiscareño-Sato

Hayward, California

Gracefully Global Group LLC
22568 Mission Blvd, No. 427
Hayward, CA 94541

State, Federal and Non-Profit Veteran-Serving Organizations, University Career Center and Student Veteran Center Directors and Corporations—Inquire about volume discounts and book the author to facilitate virtual and in-person group Personal Branding workshops by contacting us at (510) 542-9449 or *sales@GracefullyGlobal.com.*


Publisher's Cataloging-in-Publication Data
provided by Five Rainbows Cataloging Services

Name: Tiscareño-Sato, Graciela, author.
Title: B.R.A.N.D. before your resumé : your marketing guide for veterans & military service members
    entering civilian life / Graciela Tiscareño-Sato.
Description: Hayward, CA : Gracefully Global Group, 2020.
Identifiers: LCCN 2020917532 (print) | ISBN 978-0-9973090-7-2 (hardcover) | ISBN 978-0-9973090-6-
    5 (paperback) | ISBN 978-0-9973090-5-8 (ebook)
Subjects: LCSH: Veterans--Employment--United States. | Veteran reintegration--United States. |
    Career changes. | Job hunting. | Branding (Marketing) | BISAC: BUSINESS & ECONOMICS /
    Careers / Job Hunting. | BUSINESS & ECONOMICS / Marketing / General.
Classification: LCC UB357 .T57 2020 (print) | LCC UB357 (ebook) | DDC 650.14086/970973--dc23.


ISBN PDF: 978-0-9973090-8-9
ISBN ebook:  978-0-9973090-9-6

Cover photo: by Genro Sato, at Mather Air Force Base, on author's Undergraduate Navigator Training (UNT) Graduation Day

Cover Design by Kerry Watson
Interior Design by Tracy Atkins
Edited by Sarah Maples, Air Force veteran and Founder of Sarah Maples LLC
Printed in the United States of America

# Dedication

I dedicate *B.R.A.N.D. Before Your Resumé* to the thousands of service members, veterans, and military spouses I have trained coast-to-coast at conferences, on colleges campuses, and in individual coaching sessions:

Thank you for stepping up to learn the art of AUTHENTIC Personal Branding. It's not easy for us humble folks, who dedicated our lives to service of country as young adults, to learn to convey our self-worth to others.

Thank you for stepping up to *own* and *communicate* your tremendous, forward-looking value to the world.

Thank you—once you decided who you want to become for the next phase of your life—for asking me to connect you to people in my professional network, who are ready and eager to open those doors for you.

And *thank you* for trusting me to be your teacher and consultant during your military-to-civilian transition, a tumultuous, confusing, overwhelming phase of life I remember all too well.

I was happy to remind you that you are all ROCK STARS and VALUABLE LEADERS and that doesn't change the moment you hang up the uniform.

May you never settle. Please, instead, B.R.A.N.D.—before creating a resumé or anything else like a LinkedIn profile. Because you must first know yourself *and your value* before telling the world about it.

**B**ecome

**R**elevant

**A**uthentic

**N**oticeable

**D**ifferentiated

…as you reenter civilian life, and for the career transitions that will follow.

# Contents

# VETERANS: IN THEIR WORDS

Here is some of the praise veterans have had for the AUTHENTIC Personal Branding process they've learned through my live and virtual workshops, the process *you* will learn in this book:

"Graciela, I have the job, and I start in August with Intel! Thanks again for the help. Speaking with you really did help me get this internship. I read out loud the ways to describe myself, and they loved it. People need to hear you! No way you can nail your dream company without the info on branding you teach."

*—Raul Zarate, U.S. Marine Corps veteran,*
*Class of 2021, Portland State University, Oregon*

"Your workshop helped me to see the ways in which my military experience can be related to my (completely different) future career. I definitely recommend this experience to other students...especially student veterans. Developing a 'personal brand' is beneficial to anyone at any stage in their life/career, as it highlights the importance of marketing yourself, and you realize that marketing does not mean bragging!"

*—Marissa Rock, U.S. Air Force veteran*
*and student at UNC-Chapel Hill, North Carolina*

"I recently lost my job and walked into the seminar with little confidence and feeling defeated. Graciela taught me to accentuate my true authentic self, my personality, my varied skills, how to make myself and my resumé be memorable (in a positive way), the value of networking and making that personal connection with employers. When Graciela saw another veteran or me stuck on something, she easily guided us through it, to help us see it in a different and positive way. I walked out of the seminar feeling a lot more confident and looking forward to using what I learned from Graciela to find a wonderful and fulfilling new position."

*—Denise K., U.S. Army veteran, CalVet Women*
*Veterans Employment seminar, Dublin, California*
*(Denise secured a position with a state agency a few weeks later.)*

"Graciela's energy is contagious. Her dedication to the veteran community is undeniable. I had the pleasure of hosting a personal branding workshop for our student veterans during our Fall semester. Her commitment to ensuring that every student veteran understood the importance of a personal brand was impressive, but the fact that she sat with every single student to help them create their story was even more impressive. I highly recommend this workshop, and I can't wait to work with her again."

*—Justine Evirs, U.S. Navy veteran and military spouse,*
*Veteran Services Program Coordinator,*
*College of San Mateo, San Mateo, California*

"The Personal Branding Seminar led by Ms. Graciela Tiscareño-Sato was absolutely instrumental to helping veterans understand their real value!

Far too often do service men and women leave the military not fully understanding their true impact and how their individual contributions made a difference. They mask the very characteristics that enabled them to go above and beyond for their country behind their own humility and selflessness, and as a result, miss out on many opportunities. I have witnessed this as a reoccurring pattern in many veterans transitioning back into academia and later out into the workforce.

Graciela's coaching was _unique_ in that it addressed this problem directly. She instituted a _personalized_ solution for each individual in attendance. She utilized her own knowledge and military experience to personally connect with every veteran and approached each situation as if it were her own. Using expert communication skills, Graciela assisted each and every individual with breaking down their own history, putting it in perspective, and aligning it toward their future goals.

Graciela helped a room full of veterans self-actualize their own worth, while also equipping them with the communication skills they need to demonstrate that worth and accomplish their dreams. Her training was a truly valuable experience, one that every transitioning veteran should learn!"

*—Mitchell Craddock, President of the Texas A&M*
*University Veterans Association, College Station, Texas*

"We were so fortunate to have you dedicate your time to our Pacific Northwest Regional Student Veterans Conference. Your seminars on personal branding for our veteran students were exceptional. All of us came out more confident and skilled in selling ourselves. I appreciate your personal approach with each participant and wouldn't hesitate serving as a reference for anyone looking to invite you to one of their events."

*—Jason Nierman, U.S. Army veteran and Director, Military and Veteran Services, University of Idaho, Moscow, Idaho*

"Thank you for the help in thinking through the branding process. Breaking down marketing into an easy process to think through our own personal brand while addressing all of my fears was amazing in such a short seminar. Your energy is infectious!"

*—Shaun McAndrew, U.S. Navy veteran, former Professor of Naval Science and Commanding Officer, University of Idaho/Washington State University*

*Many more testimonials are available in the Recommendations section of the author's LinkedIn profile.*

# Introduction

Joining the civilian workforce is almost the exact opposite of starting active duty service.

The moment we joined our first military training unit, the institution stripped us all of our individual identity. We kept our name, but the rest of us was forced into compliance and sameness—the latter a synonym for "uniform," what we must wear to become part of that unit.

We were taught a team-and-mission-first mindset. We were taught highly-specialized, technical knowledge. Our personal values, opinions, and accomplishments were subjugated. The transition from a civilian to a military person was done to us gradually, over months and years of standardized training, led by instructors who were experts in the roles we were learning.

Conversely, when we leave the service and start preparing for our post-military careers, that training is brief, highly varied, and *not* taught by people skilled in functional roles and industries we wish to *pursue*. That exit training is typically inadequate.

We're unprepared for the civilians who expect us to talk about ourselves, who want to know about *our* leadership traits, *our* results, *our* achievements. This expectation is placed on us at a time during the transition when most service members and veterans do not feel like individuals *at all*.

During job interviews, many of us may be asked a question like, "Tell me about a time you solved a problem."

It's a question we are likely to answer with, "There was this day in Iraq when *my team and I...*"

We're literally institutionalized, still part of the collective. We struggle to articulate our individual self-worth.

I know this firsthand because I did it several times during my first interviews: "My crew and I had just taken off from Mildenhall Air Base when suddenly we lost our cabin pressurization..."

The interviewer interrupted me—"I asked about a time *you* solved a problem. I'm not interviewing your crew."

Yeah. It's tough. The struggle is very real, and I understand it.

I believe that this stark contrast—this harsh reality of how we perceive ourselves and how we define our very identity versus how we're expected to—is at the root of *why* so many of us struggle to transition into civilian life.

As our military paychecks stop coming, we are forced to remake ourselves.

But few of us leave the military with the critical mindset and skillset required to communicate a *new* identity to those who need to hear about us and offer job interviews: the marketing mindset and the art of personal branding.

What is a personal brand?

I define it this way: **Your authentic personal brand is the *differentiated* story you *intentionally* tell to attract *specific* people to you.**

But here's the problem: nobody teaches this core marketing skill to military service members *before* they transition!

There are no required courses in *how to* create a differentiated self-marketing strategy.

Nobody shows up to teach you *how to* sell yourself as the ideal candidate for a given job opening.

You're not taught *how to* extract "product attributes" to create messages that position you as the must-interview candidate in the minds of recruiters and corporate HR screeners.

Nothing like this is required before you leave active duty because the fine people who create and present TAP/Transition GPS/(insert acronym du jour here) content for transition classes are NOT marketing professionals.

And guess what? The entire job-seeking process you're beginning now for the first time, or the second or third time after a layoff, is one giant marketing exercise.

Those *non-marketing* professionals typically instruct (some have said "force") you, and other soon-to-be-veterans, to create a resumé—an externally-facing *marketing* deliverable using marketing language—*before* you know *anything* about marketing and branding!

Asking veterans to create a resumé (a marketing deliverable) *first* is like tasking someone to create a product launch website before they know anything about the product being launched!

Can you imagine doing this? Without knowing what product attributes matter to their audience, or even who the audience is that they're marketing to, you're supposed to create a website?

You would never do this to someone marketing a product that's expected to make an emotional connection with an audience to get them to buy.

Yet that's *exactly* what is done to transitioning service members *every day*.

"Create your resumé!" or "Get your LinkedIn profile set up!" they say.

No. Thou shall NOT create marketing deliverables without doing the messaging work first.

That's just wasting time and energy—a recipe for failure and frustration.

This is what I want you to avoid.

This is where I, as a veteran turned marketing professional, who lived through the hell of transition and its chaotic sense of identity loss, decide to step in and stop the madness.

You must *Brand BEFORE Your Resumé!*

It's *imperative* you get the order right—sooner instead of later.

That's why I created the **B.R.A.N.D.** acronym:

**B**ecome

  **R**elevant

   **A**uthentic

    **N**oticeable

     **D**ifferentiated

As you enter civilian life and seek meaningful employment that matches your values, you must first create a message, a personal branding story so compelling and interesting that it *grabs* the attention of the right people so that they will *ask* for your resumé. You must:

**B**ecome
**R**elevant to the audience you need to attract to connect you with the opportunities you seek. You must craft messages that are
**A**uthentic, not bragging or exaggerating, but you must be willing to be seen, to become intentionally
**N**oticeable, online, offline, to other people, and your messaging must be
**D**ifferentiated from others vying for attention in the marketplace.

THIS is marketing—grabbing the mind of others with something that's unique and fascinating.

Learning these marketing skills *now* will serve you (and others you can help) to attract professional networking contacts, informational interviews, and job interviews. The skills you will learn here will serve you for <u>decades</u>.

I will teach you a *process* that marketers use to craft powerful messages that get results. You'll be able to use this process again and again for *all* of your future career transitions, planned or otherwise. You'll also be able to implement these techniques if you launch an entrepreneurial venture, as so many veterans and military spouses do.

The content in this book is based on workshops I have spent years developing, and which have helped *thousands* of veterans to develop their personal branding to achieve their post-military goals.

I will guide you through the process of crafting your authentic, differentiated personal brand, targeted for whoever *you* need to influence into taking action on your behalf.

Like my online course, "AUTHENTIC Personal Branding for Military Veterans," this book is separated into three modules and includes the highly- effective Extracting Product Attributes Exercise, which is how you'll collect valuable words you *may* wish to use in your branding.

You'll see actual personal branding statements created by veterans during live and virtual workshops. These examples will help inspire you as you draft your own differentiated, targeted personal branding to achieve *your* next goal.

I'll start by telling you my story of how I became comfortable doing this because, believe me, I was super uncomfortable for a long time.

I will show you ample examples of great personal branding, crafted by military veterans, so you can see that there are people *just like you* doing this well. The examples will include personal branding that student veterans came up with DURING live workshops at conferences and on college campuses. (I have changed some of the names to pseudonyms to protect their privacy unless I got their permission to use actual names.)

In the second part, I will take you through an exercise to begin to create *your* brand. I will help you brainstorm unique material ("extract product attributes") from different aspects of your life. After the brainstorming, you will identify *your* target audience—who do you need to influence today for the next chapter of your life to begin?

We'll do this activity so that your brand will have *unique* value. It'll be authentic and include memorable, powerful words that tell an unforgettable story about *you*. Then you can practice getting comfortable with this new branding. I'll also teach you what *not* to do.

In the third part, I'll help you understand key connections about the art of networking—what it really is, how to do it effectively, and how to get the results that you seek. I will offer you the chance to expand your network through mine, and teach you how to set up and conduct informational interviews. That way, you can put your new branding to use right away. I'll also make myself available to help you tailor your brand for specific opportunities.

I've seen plenty of veterans write amazing personal brands using this process. *You can do this.*

I know, however, that *collaboration* is a key part of the branding process. Nobody expects you to create great branding all alone, especially for yourself the first time you're doing it.

Toward the end of the book, you'll have the option to connect with me for a private one-on-one coaching session, during which I'll review your "product attributes" list and help you polish your drafted personal branding statement.

This is exactly how we do it in every live and virtual workshop. I help each person one-on-one because personal branding is *personal*. I'm available to help you *get it done* and *ready to use wherever you need it.*

Plus, once you're ready to try your new branding and to schedule informational interviews, if you ask me via LinkedIn, I will connect you to at least one contact in my professional network. These are the people, many of whom are also veterans, who can move *your* life forward.

These are the steps that worked splendidly during my transition:

1. learn to communicate your forward-looking value (branding)
2. get comfortable introducing yourself and your value using powerful words describing your new identity (branding and networking)
3. call professionals to test your messaging and learn about their roles (branding and networking)
4. get connected to civilian employers who can't wait to learn more about you because the referral they received about you was so intriguing (branding and networking).

That's my goal for you: to help you market your value—to help you B.R.A.N.D.—so that your networking is targeted, efficient, and successful. Let's begin!

"I am Peter, aspiring ocean engineer with a track record of being motivated to seek additional training to provide increasingly better service, beginning during my career as a Navy corpsman.

Whether writing code for a MATLAB-based mapping project to enhance URI's community outreach recruiting, building a home for a military family with Team Rubicon veteran volunteers, or studying to become a future renewable energy professional, I'm constantly focused on acquiring more knowledge. I want to be part of the solution to help build a better future for all of us.

I look forward to contributing my technical skills, my love of teamwork, and my initiative to become your next ocean engineer."

—*Peter Maranan., U.S. Navy veteran, student at University of Rhode Island, Providence, Rhode Island*

# Chapter 1

## My Transition Story

Before we get started on how *you* can do it, I think it's only fair that I share my story of how I successfully transitioned from the military flight deck into a corporate marketing role in Silicon Valley—and the obstacles I overcame along the way.

The struggle, getting through it, and coming out thriving on the other side in a completely unrelated career and industry (with the help of others) is why I'm devoted to helping you today with this process, rooted in marketing skills, that works.

It's a story about how a military aviator became the creator and facilitator of *AUTHENTIC Personal Branding for Military Veterans* (and military spouses) workshops coast-to-coast who serves her fellow veterans and service members in transition.

It's a story about the women veterans and their networks who surrounded me and gave me invaluable advice missing from the standard TAP experience.

It's a story about learning how to grab recruiters' attention at a job fair, getting interviewed immediately—*without* a resumé—and then, after that, being asked to submit a resumé for second-round interviews.

It's a story about how I turned these experiences into *your* marketing guide and how you, too, can learn to B.R.A.N.D. *Before Your Resumé.*

## End of an Era

Career transitions are a phase we must go through as life happens to us. Sometimes career change is forced upon us; many times, we choose the change because we want to go in a different direction. This is what you're doing now, as you leave the armed forces, and it's what I did, too.

In my twenties and early thirties, I wore the flight suit (and blue uniform) of an Air Force officer and aviator, serving in the active duty force for nearly a decade. I decided to separate from active duty service less than a year before my major's board. Why? My engineer husband Genro Sato and I wanted to return to California, where we had met as students at Cal Berkeley. We both wanted to work in Silicon Valley as technology professionals. This would mean a major career change for me, from military aviator to corporate professional.

Having joined the active duty Air Force soon after my university graduation, I had *never* worked in the tech industry. I began to inventory what additional skills I needed to learn to make that huge jump, while I was enrolled in graduate school. (In my final two years in the service, I finished my master's degree in international business management, with an emphasis in global marketing.)

My transition timing was interesting. Six months before my separation date, I was on a special duty assignment, working for the

U.S. Embassy in Quito, Ecuador. During my lunch breaks, I interviewed many corporate telecommunications network executives for my thesis research, focused on the state of the telecom industry in Ecuador. These professionals worked at global telecom companies headquartered in Spain, Italy, the USA, and Korea. These executives kickstarted my professional network of global business leaders.

Using my Spanish language skills, I was able to follow leads provided by these industry executives about which high-level Ecuadorian government officials I should also interview for my thesis. I learned about the telecom auction process that had failed to attract foreign investment into Ecuador; along the way, I became excited about possibly working in this intriguing, strategic industry.

I also felt *terrified* of what that career transition would look like for me with no industry experience and coming from a military aviation role. More importantly, these appointments gave me a peek at what it might be like to one day interview with corporate professionals as a job seeker.

See, like most military veterans who went into active duty military service immediately after a graduation (from high school for the enlisted corps and from university in my case), I had *never* been through the type of job interview process that adults go through when they start working full time at age 18 or 22.

My knowledge gap was huge! It felt like an eternity of learning, and I felt so silly, not knowing what civilians appeared to already know.

I know I would've spiraled into depression during the heavy lift the transition process was for me if I hadn't had help. Thankfully, fellow navigator Captain Justine Tanabe, who separated six months before me, introduced me to Julia Hubbel and the women of the Hubbel Group in Spokane, Washington, where I was stationed.

## Julia to the Rescue

I was blessed to be aided by Julia Hubbel, an Army veteran. Working with mentors in the Hubbel Group, I began to learn all I didn't know. Her Hubbel Group helped me confidently network my way into my first post-military career.

The first thing Julia and her amazing group of women taught me was: "Do NOT create a resumé until you know *what in the hell you want to do next.* If you don't know what you're seeking, how can you *possibly* decide what to put into your resumé?"

Their advice provided me with great clarity. I did *not* waste time with untargeted resumé writing, even though the TAP people on base were pushing me to create one. All I created during TAP was a master list of my responsibilities, titles, projects, and educational credentials. It was *not* a resumé.

I was being guided by my civilian girlfriends (who clearly knew better than the TAP staff) to instead do the *introspective* work first. Step one was a self-assessment with a career coach to nail down the type of work I wanted to do next...to understand what work I would find fulfilling and where (organizationally) I would thrive.

They assured me that, eventually, I could create a resumé that meant something to someone, once I knew what type of work I wanted to pursue. That could only happen *after* I understood what types of corporate functions existed, entailed, and paid.

Clearly, writing a resumé was *not* the first step to take.

I began to do many informational interviews. Julia and her team taught me *how* to call industry professionals from whom I wanted to learn. They taught me *how* to persuade strangers to take time to talk to me and *how* to learn all I wanted to know from this person and their professional role. They taught me *how* to continuously grow my network.

Working with mentors in the Hubbel Group, I learned how to introduce myself in such a way at job fairs that the listener became totally intrigued and just HAD to interview me.

In other words, I learned how to craft my personal branding and used it very successfully. And I practiced being interviewed—a LOT.

I heard dozens of both terrific and ridiculous questions employers ask during interviews. I learned how to answer those interview questions honestly. I learned which responses yielded positive results and which answers totally bombed.

I squirmed at the question "What are some of your strengths?" because I felt forced to say positive, wonderful things about myself.

See, that felt totally against the nature of being a humble military officer (and a Latina and a Catholic woman…so much social programming behind those feelings, as you'll see later on).

Remember, I went straight from college graduation to undergraduate navigator training (UNT). No job interview was required; I had signed a contract with the Air Force as a scholarship cadet while in college. At the age of 32, and as an unemployed civilian, I was literally playing catch up. I was learning what others my age had learned a decade before and had already mastered.

I was super uncomfortable having to substantiate my ability to work with people in teams, on the ground. Because "working in an office setting is very different than working in an airplane," one guy told me during an interview.

I did not at all appreciate having to explain the value I might bring to an organization in an industry in which I had zero work experience. I felt like I was speculating at best (totally bullshitting at worst) when forced to answer that question.

I remember feeling resentful at having to defend my decision to serve on active duty—made worse each time I was reminded that I had "no industry experience" for the position for which I had applied.

The problem that I didn't know I had at the time (that nearly 100% of transitioning service members have) was this: *I did not know how to communicate my value.*

I did not know how to separate the results of the work I had done and why it mattered from the abhorrent concept of "talking about myself." I had zero comfort with the act of telling people about my professional achievements, leadership positions during deployments, community service work while on active duty, and the numerous awards I had received for Outstanding this or that. I minimized my string of achievements by thinking, "that was just my job."

If you're reading this now and you've just hung up your uniform (or soon will), you know *exactly* what I'm talking about.

With the mentorship of Julia and her amazing group of women (including role-playing mock job interviews with me), I received multiple job offers from a variety of industries. I was flown to corporate headquarters offices to meet senior executives I would work with *if* I accepted the offer in hand. In one city, I was even paired with a real estate agent for a day. He showed me fancy new homes I could buy with my new, tempting corporate marketing professional salary.

I treated myself to six months of professional development work. I was happy to collect unemployment insurance payments for the first time in my life to give myself that time to learn. I thought of it as a how-to-operate-as-a-civilian-in-search-of-a-paycheck experience—something I had never done before.

That personal assessment I did to understand my *values* and *interests* was as a 32-year-old married woman with no children. Honestly, that self-assessment exercise felt truly foreign and uncomfortable, coming from the military flight deck where crewmembers are *never* asked about values and interests. You just do the thing you're trained to do.

During this time, I turned down ALL job offers I received.

The truth is this: the positions were with companies I had *no* interest in working for, but enjoyed getting to know about as I learned to master job interviews.

In the live and virtual workshops I facilitate, I get specific about the recruiting organization that was trying to place me with *their* corporate clients in whatever positions were open. The career in the telecommunications industry, which I'd stated I wanted, mattered to *none* of those recruiters. In fact, one recruiter told me straight up that "Nobody is going to hire you for a marketing position in a telecom firm because you have no industry experience." Seriously.

Here's how it worked: after placing a candidate into one of those positions their clients had open, the recruiter would get compensated a full third of my salary (as I found out later in the process.) I felt they were trying to use me, so I was fine using them to practice what I needed to master. (Ask me more in a live chat. I'll name names.)

Recruiting agencies won't tell you how much their clients will pay their recruiters (it's a percentage of your negotiated salary) when you accept a position, so if you're curious, go ahead and ask. I was so naïve, and I didn't ask until much later. I believe in transparency.

Eventually, I was hired for *exactly* the job I imagined existed… without a recruiter…tapping my network.

I connected with the hiring manager directly by emailing alumni friends from Berkeley and describing *exactly* the role I was seeking. I did this after all those job interviews, when I was certain I wanted a global marketing role, and, very importantly, when I felt confident about the entire process.

Once I knew the type of role I wanted and could succinctly ask for help from my network, it took *five minutes* to get connected with that exact opportunity for which one of my friends was hiring. Five minutes…but after months of doing the work to be ready for *that* moment.

I was hired by German telecommunications company Siemens, headquartered in Munich, as a Global Marketing Manager in their Silicon Valley office. I *negotiated* the first offer I received from them (something, by the way, that ONLY 10% of women do!!!) and got an initial salary bump for my effort.

Once I signed the offer, I approached Julia, who was leaving Spokane the same week my husband and I were moving to California. Outside her house, as the movers packed her belongings, I thanked her profusely for her guidance, her mentorship, and her introduction to the group of women who provided me with the actual, *valuable*, unofficial Transition Assistance Program of skills that mattered.

I asked Julia, "How can I ever thank you for helping me through that chaotic transition period?"

Her answer is my fuel today: "Just pay it forward. Teach another service member what to do to become successfully employed as a civilian. Especially important: teach other women."

## Paying It Forward

After over nine years working in that first corporate marketing role at Siemens Enterprise Networks, I worked in a second industry: I was hired as the North American Marketing Manager for a foreign start-up company, a solar photovoltaic electronics company headquartered in Tel Aviv, Israel. I was responsible for strategic and product marketing, from message creation to creating marketing deliverables to industry analyst briefings and more. I helped that startup establish a footprint in Canada, Mexico, and the USA.

For the past ten years, I have been running my successful educational publishing and multicultural marketing company, Gracefully Global Group LLC. We publish the award-winning literature and digital course content I want to see in the world, to showcase the positive contributions of Latino Americans in the USA. And that body of work attracts invitations to serve a variety of customer segments, as a bilingual keynote speaker and workshop facilitator. Essentially, I'm in the business of inspiration, as a storyteller in both written and spoken form.

As I became visible on social media networks after publishing my first book, I was contacted by Army veteran Dali Rivera, at the time a student at Towson University in Baltimore. She asked me to please come to her campus to teach her and her fellow student veterans how to promote themselves and their businesses "without feeling like pompous blowhards."

That's when the AUTHENTIC Personal Branding workshop was born—at the request of student veterans who had discovered, by observing my online communications, that something was missing in their professional development toolkit.

I created the content and flew to Baltimore, where I taught multiple workshops in a day to accommodate student schedules. I recall I trained about 50 veterans in total on that visit.

When I asked them: "What is holding you back from talking about your achievements?" the student veterans talked openly about their struggles creating a new identity for themselves months after leaving the active duty force. It was a fabulous opportunity to cocreate personal branding with each of these ambitious student veterans. I found it deeply gratifying to directly serve my fellow veterans in transition.

Since that spring in 2013, I have taught thousands of student veterans, transitioning veterans in our communities (including vets completing rehab programs), other college students, and professionals *how* to craft their targeted, compelling personal brands. I teach veterans—many of whom left the service years ago and *still* had never been taught how to create their authentic personal branding. More frequently now, I also teach their entrepreneurial spouses. The workshop is a transformational experience for all attendees, as the examples you'll see throughout this book will prove.

The idea to create the B.R.A.N.D. acronym:

**B**ecome

**R**elevant

**A**uthentic

**N**oticeable

**D**ifferentiated

…came to me during an especially busy stretch of travel in the spring of 2019. I flew cross-country to teach this workshop at the University of North Carolina—Chapel Hill in late March, then up to the University of Idaho to facilitate the training at the Student Veterans of America Pacific Northwest Regional Conference, and two weeks later back up to Portland State University for two full days of training student vets there.

It hit me to finally write a book to define and teach the branding process to my fellow veterans—people who are extraordinary humans, who have been taught tons of skills, and who've mastered them all over the globe.

But the skill of creating your own powerful personal brand—by "extracting product attributes" as we marketers call that brainstorming process—and thinking about what matters to your target audience, then selecting powerful words to craft the story that will ensure people do *not* forget you...well, that skill just isn't one we were ever taught while in uniform. Not at all.

I'm going to teach you authentic personal branding for *you*, the military veteran, because you know what? Making that transition from Air Force Officer and aviator, KC-135 navigator into marketing manager for a Silicon Valley technology company—that was a *really* crazy career transition, and I learned a lot. I had a lot of guidance, a lot of strong mentoring, during that time.

Yet, I know that most veterans do not leave the service with a degree in marketing, and do not necessarily have a support group of professional businesswomen, as I did, to guide them through the process.

So I'm paying it forward by teaching authentic personal branding so that you can, as soon as you finish this book (or complete the three-module online course), begin to put together the compelling language, words, storytelling, and images to make yourself the *must-have* candidate in the job interview process during your transition.

I will demonstrate the power of creating your personal brand, whether you're a job seeker, applying to transfer to a four-year university, or launching a business, as so many veterans do.

THAT is what you're going to learn right here, with my guidance.

You'll be able to put your new branding into action *immediately* and, if you take me up on it, you'll be able to grow your net worth through my network.

You'll learn how to do informational interviews, and I'll connect you to people in my network that can help you take the next step forward—I promise this to you.

The work I do to teach *AUTHENTIC Personal Branding for Military Veterans* on university campuses, in public libraries, and in other community venues where veterans gather, online and in person, is simply keeping my promise to Julia Hubbel, the woman veteran who helped make my military-to-civilian transition a smashing success.

It mattered so much to me to trust a fellow veteran, a woman who had also undergone the military-to-civilian transition. I trusted her, and her networking group of women, completely to guide me. That same spirit is why veterans trust me to teach them this skill that nobody showed up to teach them before they separated. This is how I continue to pay it forward.

# MODULE 1

## Branding Basics

"I'm Victoria, disabled Army veteran and future entrepreneur of a community education center. I'm the jack of all trades, an education expert who organized, designed, and opened a community-based, English tutoring program for the city of Selma. Having served in Germany, South Korea, and Canada tasked with overseeing budgets, I'm a nimble leader that leads by example and loves helping people achieve their educational goals."

*—Victoria, U.S. Army veteran attendee at a CalVet Women Veterans Employment seminar in Fresno, California*

"I'm Walt, trusted counselor to multicultural communities ranging from parishioners, to hospital patients and military veterans. I've spent my life serving in diverse communities on the west coast, east coast, and Hawaii, where the US Air Force sent me. I'm the reliable programming expert you call when you need a creative leader to take ideas from conception to completion in nonprofit organizations and university settings. Whether I'm managing a housing program in Washington D.C., creating programs for student veterans, or crafting a model for civic engagement, I use my storytelling skills, both the written and spoken word, to create synergy and community.

Because I'm accustomed to attracting, organizing, and activating the most diverse citizens imaginable, I'm the ideal candidate to become your next Student Services leader."

—*Walt Ghant, U.S. Air Force veteran, attendee at a virtual workshop for Student Veterans hosted by Portland State University*

# CHAPTER 2

## The Power of Personal Branding

"I'm Marland—aspiring voice and speech sciences researcher of cognitive linguistics, with a deep curiosity for the unknown aspects of language acquisition after speech loss.

Whether leading the training and recruiting of staff while optimizing resources to improve operational efficiency, mentoring my fellow student veterans at URI, or performing in European cities with a choir, I'm the creative, selfless, collaborative influence manager constantly entrusted to lead my peers in a variety of endeavors.

I look forward to becoming your next Speech and Language Pathology researcher and one day serving individuals with speech and language disorders."

*—Marland, U.S. Army veteran and student at the University of Rhode Island, Providence, Rhode Island*

I've shared the story of what it took for me to transition from the military flight deck onboard the KC-135 refueling tanker to becoming a global marketing manager for a global tech giant with offices in

Silicon Valley. Later, I transitioned to being an entrepreneur and business owner, and an award-winning author.

I know the craziest-sounding career transitions *can* be done. I've done several. I know many veterans who have also done so...successfully.

So, please, do *not* let people tell you that a new career you want to pursue is out of reach. It is NOT.

How I did it begins with this: at each transition point, beginning with my military-to-civilian transition, I learned to articulate my *differentiated* value to influence (and attract) my new specific audience. In short, I developed my personal brand.

I didn't do this intuitively; I had to learn from others. And the steps that worked for me and that I've taught to thousands of others are now in this book.

First of all, I want you to really understand branding.

## What Is Personal Branding Anyway?

What is a brand? For those who have not studied the business discipline of marketing, I will simply say here that at the heart and soul of the marketing discipline, there are the four classic "Ps" of marketing: Product, Placement, Pricing, and Positioning.

Now, in any business school curriculum, each of these P-named concepts can be an entire course to deeply explore these elements. We're not doing that in this book (or the workshop or the online course). Nope. We're totally focused on what *you* need, *practically*, as a veteran, service member, or military spouse in transition.

Therefore, we're going to zoom right in on *Positioning*, because that's what branding is. A brand is a way to *position* yourself in my mind, in the mind of your audience. Marketers say they want to capture "mindshare," which means to occupy space in somebody's mind.

Positioning, as a practice, is also used by marketers and analysts to draw a picture of a market, to place a brand in that marketplace in a particular position—thus the act of *positioning*.

Think of the auto manufacturer market. In that example, you can draw positioning charts of brands known for inexpensive, small vehicles targeted for the college student market, medium-sized mass market minivans for families, and larger (or exotic) luxury vehicles for the super-wealthy bunch. That's helpful, in the minds of potential customers, to understand where a brand fits relative to other brands in the overall marketplace. A positioning chart shows visually how a brand compares to its competitors within a market segment. But ultimately, where it fits depends simply on how people THINK about the brand—and *that* is the work of the marketer.

To do this, to capture "mindshare," you must be clear and memorable when creating your personal brand. Because the recipient—your target audience—will classify *you* as automatically as consumers classify automaker brands.

Here's a slide to show you the classic marketing principles that I mentioned before: product, price, positioning, and promotion.

# Corporate vs. Personal Marketing

| Marketing Principle | CORPORATE | PERSONAL |
| --- | --- | --- |
| Product | Various, subject to product life cycle, ever-evolving, innovation | **You!** Can be laser-focused in one area of expertise, or multi-faceted areas of expertise. Be clear. |
| Price | Tied to perceived value, subject to competitive pressures, discounts, can lower price for one product and others "subsidize" | Depends on power of brand, **you have only one.** Do it right, your price can go up as you become more valuable.. |
| Position (in minds of target audience) | Spend tons of survey $ to measure brand awareness within target audiences (CIO, moms, etc) | Usually UNKNOWN for individuals. You must take specific steps to learn it. Media reports already influencing your audience (generalities/stereotypes.) LinkedIn recommendations help. **MESSAGE is everything.** |
| Promotion | Ideally detailed in product marketing plan and tied to strategic objectives. Subject to marketing budgets, staff creativity, whims of executives. | Puts all Ps together to execute plan. Do mini plan w/objectives, messages (A/B testing), detail tactics like: •Your social networking profiles •Your blog, website, email marketing list |

I don't intend for you to study this entire slide. I simply want to show you that these principles apply at the corporate level, the product level, and yes, at the *personal* level—because now *you* are the product for sale into a specific market!

As you become a civilian seeking employment, you're engaging in selling yourself to specific people, who are looking for specific talent and value.

If you're running a business, you're selling yourself to your prospective clients. And, of course, you want to motivate the *right* type of clients to take action to do business with you. Other client types are irrelevant to you in your branding effort.

Let me provide an example of why *clarity* of content and *focus* on a specific audience is important in branding. There are a lot of different words that can be used to describe me, as a professional. Take a look at this list:

- **Brand = <u>positioning yourself in my mind</u>**
  - My mind already knows things, categorizes people
  - Not all minds need to know the same about you
  - **Contextual!**
  - **Be MEMORABLE – <u>make me NOT forget you</u>**

i.e. Veteran, Publisher, Coach, Multicultural Marketer, Author, Speaker, Mother of Dual-Sensory Impaired Child – *but never all in one message!*

I show these words on a slide during the workshop *to intentionally overwhelm your mind* and make this point: all those words accurately apply to describe me as a professional, but I would *never* use all of those words in one branding message.

Why would I never do that? Simple. That word salad is targeted at no audience in particular; therefore, it reaches *nobody.*

As is, that list is too confusing. Your mind wouldn't know what to do with all those words, or where to position me inside your mind.

Yet, too many veterans feel compelled to say *everything* about themselves as they transition into the civilian workplace. In so doing, they confuse the market and reach nobody.

When I did that in the beginning, during my transition, it was an act of desperation. My thinking went something like this: "I have to tell potential employers every project I've done on base, off base, primary duty, additional duty, missions and projects while deployed, leadership experiences, volunteer work, everything. I have to do this because I feel deficient as a civilian candidate, yet want those recruiters and employers to think I'm good enough to compete with someone who has already been working in the industry I want to enter."

Sound familiar?

In my moments of desperation, when I tried to prove myself worthy of an interview by mindlessly including everything in my resumé and uploading it somewhere, I instead confused people who might have interviewed me. They never called me. They instead called another candidate who communicated more clearly and who reached their *mind*.

Instead of being clear about my *value* to *their organization*, I was consumed in those weak moments with trying to say everything about myself, which only resulted in *not* getting heard.

That's quite typical when you're *not* used to thinking like a marketer, as I certainly was not back then. We all tend to think of *ourselves* first instead of the *audience* we need to reach and impress! It's a mindset shift we have to make as transitioning military members.

To really position yourself in your audience's mind, the mind you're trying to influence, what I will be teaching you is how to choose words so that you occupy the space in the person's mind that you *want* to occupy. It's a very targeted, almost surgical process to cause a specific action to happen.

That, in short, is branding—a critical function of marketing. It's not all of marketing, but it is a foundational part. This is what I will be teaching you.

## Your Windshield vs. Your Rearview

Corporations spend a great deal of money to understand how their brand is currently positioned in the marketplace. In other words, they want to understand the "baseline positioning" in the minds of the people they have as customers, and in the minds of those they want to *attract* as customers. Once a company knows the brand's baseline, it can formulate plans to either strengthen the brand positioning or to take action to drive the positioning in a new direction.

The baseline positioning, when you're doing personal branding, is usually not known. You don't really know what space you occupy in someone's mind in an industry you wish to enter. Perhaps you don't occupy *any* space because they've never heard of you. Such is the case if you're looking to interview with a company that you've never been introduced to (you know nobody there and have never visited the company). This is also the case if you're marketing your company's products and services to a new market segment, where your company is unknown to decision makers.

Here's the takeaway: as a human doing personal branding work, you must take specific steps to learn what you want your personal branding to *do* for you. We undergo branding and marketing activities because we want to *motivate* someone to *do* something.

You should create your brand with the knowledge that, when you do this work, those minds you are seeking to influence *already* know things—about people similar to you. Other information is already out in the world that is influencing your audience.

For example, let me bring up media reports about military veterans and Hollywood imagery of people in uniform. Those stories and images, that have been seen by most adults, can cause minds to think they know about "people like you." It's just human nature, the need to sort people into easy-to-understand categories. It's a primal thing that humans do. Just be aware that *all* minds do this. *You* do it. *I* do it.

Think again about your intended audience, the one you want to influence: Are they hearing good things about military veterans? Are they hearing not-so-good stuff about military veterans? Are they operating with generalities or stereotypes? The answers here are likely *yes.*

These things are already lodged in the minds of the people you're trying to influence. You can't erase that information. It's part of that "baseline positioning" you need to be aware of as you start.

Your challenge then is to come up with a message that helps you to *effectively* occupy a position in those minds, to paint the image and idea *you* want to paint about yourself.

That picture you're painting may, in fact, strongly contradict what's already in their minds. If your personal branding statement is *so compelling* that it grabs their attention this way, you will capture the mindshare you want. They will *demand* to know more about you because they're intrigued! You'll know this is happening because they'll invite you to come in for an interview, if you're in a job search; they'll invite you to submit a proposal, if you're a business owner.

Staying on the topic of first learning what might already be known about you (baseline positioning), let's look at LinkedIn.

If you're already on that powerful platform for professionals, the LinkedIn recommendations section of your profile is one source of info you can reference to study what is already part of your personal brand.

What are the people who sing your praises in Recommendations saying about you and your value?

What words are they choosing to describe what you do and why it's important? Can you use parts of those descriptions to craft your brand?

During the branding brainstorming exercise we will do later in this book, I will suggest various phases of your life from where you may draw ideas as you create your new, forward-looking branding to position yourself to your intended audience. Most people are pleasantly surprised when we do this; they suddenly remember fantastic things they've accomplished, actions and projects they're proud of that they'd completely forgotten. Just wait. You'll see!

Remember this as you read any LinkedIn Recommendations you may have received from others: "We live our brand."

Done right, you are living your brand every day (if it's authentically yours)—whether you are mindful of it or not.

Let's clarify something that always comes up in the live workshops: Your *reputation* is based on events that have already happened; it's what people say and know about your past experiences.

Your authentic personal *branding*, conversely, is intentionally NEW and FORWARD-LOOKING. You create and communicate your personal branding to express what impact you want to have on events *in the future*, by telling a story that highlights something special *from your past.*

See the difference?

I love this quote from fellow veteran and recruiter Sultan Camp in one of my favorite articles about personal branding and transitioning EVER written. (You'll find the citation in the Resources section in the back of the book.)

> *"Your resumé should be a windshield*
> *document. That is, it should reflect*
> *the positions you're going towards."*

Since your resumé is a personal marketing deliverable, in which you showcase your authentic personal brand targeted at a specific audience you want to influence, this logically also applies to your *brand*. It should be crafted to be a "windshield document" to "reflect the positions you're going *toward*."

I've seen an evolution of advice that pertains to branding, reputation, and networking that is relevant here. Have you heard these tidbits throughout your professional life?

People say things like, "It's not what you know, it's who *you* know."

Or perhaps they've told you, "It's not what you know, it's *who* knows *you*."

I question that. Is it really just who I know and who knows me? Is it really that simple?

The answer is: of course not!

Authenticity matters. *What* is known about you? The *real* you?

At a networking event, for example, when your name comes up, what are they saying? Do you even know?

And how much of that which is known did YOU create and communicate about yourself?

Herein lies the difference between reputation and authentic personal branding and an understanding of where they intersect.

I love this definition that I saw at a Sustainable Brands conference several years ago, where I spoke on a panel:

"A brand is first who you are." (So again, authenticity.) "Then it's *what* you do, *how* you do it, and then *how you talk about it.*"

In your professional life, you'll likely encounter people branding themselves and including stuff they've never done. You'll hear them talking this way, and you will see right through that. You'll know it's super phony. Authenticity matters. That's why I call what we craft *AUTHENTIC* Personal Branding.

Who you are, what you do, how you do it, and then how you talk about it—in that order.

So, let's talk about you, the brand. It's *not* just "who knows you." It's what they know and say about you. It's the *content*, it's the *message* that matters!

Remember that people hire people they *like*. One way they're going to like you is because they know about you—you are known to other people who talk about you, who recommend you, who refer you, and connect you to others.

More importantly, you want to affect the content and message being used to talk about you. You want people to talk about you, your value, and what YOU want to happen *next* so that the people YOU need to reach hear your message. You want those specific people to be compelled to want to know more about you.

## Captivating Your Audience

Now let's take a big step closer to understanding the power of awesome personal branding by studying some examples, as I promised you earlier.

Here's the first one: a woman named Marta, who is living her personal brand, unlike anybody I've ever met.

I met businesswoman Marta at a VIP dinner the night before a business conference for women in San Francisco. As the award recipient and keynote speaker, I was fortunate to be introduced to all event sponsors.

When Marta approached me, she took my hand in hers and said, "Hi, I'm Marta, the non-smear lipstick lady."

Then she kissed the back of my hand!

She said, "My lipstick never smears, see?"

I looked down, and, of course, the lipstick she was wearing had *not* stained my hand.

Wow! That was some seriously differentiated messaging right there!

Marta had introduced herself with a very powerful personal brand, one that included the value to me, while also introducing her product line. That moment has never left me, and I assure you that I will *never* forget her.

The next day at the conference, I sought out her booth and loved her wonderful exhibit.

# Living her Personal Brand

Marta, the lipstick lady –**DIFFERENTIATED** herself with a kiss

Marta expertly blended her personal branding, her product line, and her corporate branding at her booth. Look at the tote bag she has—it has lips all over it! She's got the banner with the non-smear lipstick website. *Everything* reinforces her authentic personal branding with which she introduced herself when she kissed my hand and called herself "Marta, the non-smear lipstick lady."

Even though I rarely wear lipstick, I eagerly became her customer and purchased several products for myself and for my sister, who wears lipstick daily. I was *that* intrigued by Marta and her unique personal branding.

Most importantly, the way she introduced herself to me at the dinner told me a story in a way that I'll *never forget*. That is compelling, unforgettable personal branding. That is a powerful example of really living your personal branding.

What can YOU do to craft a personal brand so unique that people remember it years later?

As a business owner, what story can *you* tell that will make people want to continue buying from you again and again?

Here's another example of terrific personal branding: a friend of mine, Darlene, sells these Christmas ornaments made of glass, all with a strong Latinx heritage celebration reflected in the designs. She attended one of my very first personal branding workshops for professionals in Silicon Valley. In the one-on-one session, I told her that the designs were so cool, and she should consider doing a little feature on her website about the people who created the designs because they're so unique.

That's when she looked at me, and she said, "Graciela, *I* designed all those ornaments. *I'm* the designer."

I looked at her in surprise and replied, "You know what? Nothing on your CasaQ website tells us that *you* are the designer genius of these beautiful ornaments!"

As is typical of too many entrepreneurs, Darlene was only showcasing product, product, product. She had never told her potential buyers *her* story about *her* role as a designer and entrepreneur. Darlene later revamped her website and put herself squarely in the middle of her creative work. In so doing, she made an important and *authentic* emotional connection with potential buyers.

This woman has been wildly successful—Darlene has had her ornaments distributed at the Latin Grammy's. Macy's sells them. Celebrities love them.

Darlene *finally* put herself into her story as a central character, next to her products, and told us the fascinating journey she's lived developing her brand, her products, and her company.

See, here's the truth: People are much more likely to buy from you (or interview you for a job opening) once you've captivated them with the story of *you*—because *you* can be a powerful, attention-grabbing brand.

In fact, you will NOT get scheduled for a job interview UNTIL you've captured some mindshare and grabbed someone's attention, until you've successfully risen above the fray, until you've differentiated yourself from other candidates.

That's simply the way it works with humans and buying / interviewing decisions. The job-seeking and interviewing process is simply one long marketing exercise.

You'll find success by developing *your* personal brand, to influence exactly the audience you need to attract.

I love this example because it's so relatable to us as veterans. Too many times, especially when starting a business, we *don't* want to tell our story.

You're uncomfortable speaking about *yourself*, right?

Maybe you outright resist doing so?

I know—early on, I did, too.

You want it to be all about the services and the products you want to sell. But *you* are the story, and that's very important as part of this personal branding work.

I want you to appreciate the power of your personal story, not only in transitioning for your first corporate position (or whatever you're trying to do after you leave the service), but also if you answer that strong call to become an entrepreneur, as many do in our veteran and military spouse community.

I want you to have a *strong* awareness of this power. Know that, if the entrepreneurial spirit comes for you, that *you* are the brand. Everything you're learning now, as you become a civilian, as you develop your authentic personal brand, will help you later as an entrepreneur. This knowledge has helped me, and it has helped so many others.

Now that I've shown you two examples of powerful, differentiated personal branding, let me switch over and show you *veterans* doing personal branding in a very powerful way.

Here is my first example. I'm going to show you a series of slides, showing how this woman veteran evolved her personal branding.

Pay attention to her focus, her specificity in word choices and images, as she reaches for different audiences as her personal and professional needs change. Understand this example because that's what *you* are ultimately going to do—create a brand you may wish to represent with words *and* visuals (especially so if you use any social media platform).

I'll demonstrate to you that HOW and WHERE you decide to tell your story will depend on the *audience* you are attempting to attract.

For each specific audience type, you might choose different words and different images to emphasize your key messages.

Let's meet Eve. Eve found me after I left the stage at the end of the Personal Branding Panel at the Women Veterans Career Development Conference in Arlington, Virginia. Eve asked me to look at her Twitter account and offer constructive criticism for improvement. This is what her Twitter account looked like in 2014 while she served in the Navy Reserves and aboard the USS Enterprise.

# A Veteran's Brand EVOLVES

You can see that at that time, still on active duty, Eve was showcasing her military service, her "visionary badass" brand, and her "changemaker" language. She also branded herself as a Jewish U.S. Navy Veteran. Look at the words she chose for her profile: *executive director* of a couple of organizations, *founder* of something else, *cofounder* of something else.

Her intent here was to show us her unique, feminine power as a woman in uniform, preparing to exit the armed forces. Like most service members in transition, who create social media profiles, it's not apparent which audience Eve was hoping to reach with this early personal branding.

In addition to being a "badass," Eve, like so many of us veterans, decided later to launch a small business. Eve is an educated professional with accounting and finance skills; she wanted to attract small business owners in need of these critical business services.

So Eve created another Twitter handle called QuickBooks Badass.

## Veterans Branded—Twitter
## *Accountant & Biz Owner*

There she is with the picture you saw before—that strong physical pose; she kept that half of her brand. However, to begin to attract a *specific* audience, she changed the wording and imagery in her profile.

She created a different version of her personal brand, this time designed to capture the attention of *small business owners* who might need bookkeeping services.

In this evolving version of her personal brand, for the *new* audience she wanted to attract, Eve showcased her Intuit certifications. She's certified as a ProAdvisor for QuickBooks, accounting software that helps business owners manage the very important function of bookkeeping. (All businesses need a trusted bookkeeper, and while Eve's not my bookkeeper, I do have a bookkeeper who is an Intuit certified ProAdvisor as well, so I appreciate what Eve did here.) Eve selected different words, showcased Certified QuickBooks ProAdvisor, and ditched the picture of her standing on the aircraft carrier, which was not relevant to this *new* audience in need of bookkeeping services.

*Different* words for a *different* purpose to attract a *different* audience, yet she kept the "badass" piece. That piece says, "I am powerful, I am knowledgeable, I can get this done for you."

Indeed—Why hire a regular bookkeeper when you can hire a bookkeeping BADASS?

I really love how she evolved that branding.

Guess what happened next? Eve decided to run for political office. Let's look at her Twitter feed during the campaign:

## Veterans Branded—Twitter
### *Candidate for Office*

Eve kept the language to communicate she's a Navy veteran, yes—because she figured it would appeal to voters. To attract an even wider set of voters, she revealed she's a mother, founder of a couple of organizations, and, most importantly, a candidate in District 33 for the Maryland State Senate. Clearly, she was building a following of people who would support her candidacy for elected office.

As I reviewed this manuscript for the final time before heading into production, I had to go check on Eve's Twitter profile again, since it had been a few years. I learned she had just become an ordained minister, and, sure enough, she had updated her personal branding to communicate her most recent message of faith and feminine power! Here it is:

# Veterans Branded—Twitter
## *Ordained minister & combat veteran*

**Maven Eve**
@RevMavenEve

Mother. Interfaith minister. Combat veteran. Activist. Finance nerd. Nonprofit Buff. Empath. Vocalist. #NormalizeLove #MatriarchyRising #BlackLivesMatter

⊙ Maryland, USA    ▦ Joined March 2014

I show you these examples so you can see how the words and images that *you* select for your branding can indeed evolve as *your* interests and professional goals evolve.

With each variant, Eve was expecting to attract a *different* audience.

Eve is a great example of this point: choose the personal branding you need for the audience you need to influence *now*, knowing that in the future, this may change, because *you* may change. You're human. It's going to happen!

Here's the takeaway from this section: I'm teaching you in this book, in the workshop, and in the online course, a *repeatable process.* You'll now always be equipped to repeat this branding process whenever it's time to evolve *your* branding for a new purpose and a new audience.

## A Peek at My Personal Branding

You might be curious, so I'll show you my personal branding on the social media network I use most often:

LinkedIn ( *https://www.linkedin.com/in/gracielatiscarenosato/* ).

It's my life's work to be an inspirational storyteller, motivating people to live their best lives by living unusually.

Today, I share my love of the U.S. Air Force with children, their parents, and their teachers as a bilingual author and publisher. That's why we created the award-winning Captain Mama children's book series through the publishing firm I founded.

Notice that on my LinkedIn profile, I intentionally chose words to attract K through 12 educators, the primary market segment for the award-winning literature products my company Gracefully Global

Group creates. University customers and libraries also buy our books, but, in *this* branding, I want to attract *primary* market segments.

You see me there with several middle school-aged girls, who tried on my flight suits during a school visit. I shared my story of being the daughter of immigrants (as many of the students in that community also are), a U.C. Berkeley graduate, and an Air Force officer and aviator turned businesswoman and author. I *love* that photo I chose for my profile. It supports my personal branding as a role model for young women and girls.

Part of my unique personal branding is that blend: I want educators looking at my profile to immediately connect me in their minds with their *students*—to imagine the impact my literature and a live presentation can have in *their* classrooms.

In other words, my personal branding is designed to communicate benefits to my *audience*…ALWAYS. It's not about me. My personal branding communicates my *value* to a *specific* audience. You'll see additional examples of that in my profile narrative (About section) on LinkedIn.

I want someone looking at my profile to know in two seconds that I'm committed to being a bilingual public speaker and positive role model for kids, that I create powerful literature as a publisher, and that I consult with school districts. I selected specific words to communicate *those* ideas because *those* are the audiences I want to attract and to call me. My audience will notice these words and understand the value I can deliver in their schools.

Importantly, I'm on LinkedIn because many educators connect with other educators and community partners like me on this platform. (It's a close second to Instagram as the best way to connect with teachers.)

In fact, I'm deliberate about which social media platforms to contribute to because I don't join networks willy nilly. Every platform can become a giant time suck.

Instead, I study where my audience is online and which social media communities they prefer. I then show up and communicate my AUTHENTIC Personal Branding to attract *those* specific people. If I were trying to attract a different audience, I would use different words.

I'm emphasizing this point because, as we wrap up this first section and get into the branding activity, I want you to keep in mind that *who you are trying to reach* must be clear in your mind BEFORE you make any decisions about the words you wish to communicate. *This is paramount.*

If you're a student veteran and you're looking for your first job after graduation, you are trying to attract corporate HR professionals and recruiters. You want them to see your unique value, get motivated to learn more about you, and invite you to send your resumé—because your personal branding goal is to *intrigue this audience to secure an interview.* That's it.

Here's a powerful personal branding example from a student veteran who did just that. Raul was part of a virtual group training with one-to-one coaching earlier this year:

"I'm Raul, lifelong technology tinkerer—the go-to-person for family members, fellow students and faculty members when they get stuck understanding their technology.

As a young Marine, I was entrusted to repair electronics, prepare and maintain aircraft to fly, and other flight-line operations. Today my curiosity as a self-motivated computer engineer has me programming in three different computer languages and building computers for myself and family. My years as a role model, motivating young people and family members to pursue STEM education and careers, in addition to my open-minded innovator mindset, make me an astounding candidate for the _____ Apprenticeship."

*—Raul Zarate, U.S. Marine Corps veteran,*
*Portland State University, Class of 2021, Portland, Oregon*

Raul used this branding to secure an interview with Intel. He wrote to me after accepting the job offer to say that the Intel recruiter loved how he described himself and his value.

When you're in this phase of your job search, your audience also includes corporate employees working at major corporate brands who have titles like "Manager, Military Talent Recruiting" or "Program Manager, Military Advocacy."

(By the way, before you read that, did you even know these job titles existed inside corporations? I didn't when I was transitioning!)

As a candidate, you want to attract both corporate and independent recruiters and hiring managers too. Your target audience is generally *professionals who are actively seeking to hire and place military veterans with specific skill sets.*

You're working to create a personal brand that attracts an audience very different from my audience of K through 12 educators. I'll remind you about this need for *audience targeting* in the next section.

"I'm Jared, a civil engineering student at Portland State. While working at Union Pacific as a conductor, I became fascinated by the feats of civil engineering that made the railroad possible. While serving as a combat advisor in the Middle East, I used my tenacity and creative problem-solving skills to teach and mentor host-country soldiers on complex tasks by overcoming linguistic and cultural barriers. I look forward to bringing my skills and experience to your engineering firm and projects."

—*Jared, U.S. Marine Corps veteran and student at Portland State University, Portland, Oregon*

# MODULE 2

## YOUR Personal Brand

"I'm Lisha, a recent information technology graduate and Navy veteran, who built networks on military ships. I've been an information systems security manager and have cybersecurity experience. Whether I'm building networks on ships or mentoring children in the community, I look forward to using my leadership, problem-solving, and technical skills to make an impact on your organization."

—Lisha, U.S. Navy veteran, attended CalVet-sponsored "AUTHENTIC Personal Branding" workshop for women veterans at Operation Dress Code conference, San Diego, California

# CHAPTER 3

## To Create Your Personal Brand Is to Look *Forward*

"I'm Omowunmi, aspiring federal agency employee (ideally USDA or SSA) with deep experience managing both military personnel and civilian contractor relationships while deployed with the U.S. Army. Whether I'm composing gospel music, persuading community members to join our church, or managing my soldiers' post deployment leave, my attention to detail and energy are always front and center.

I'm the go-to person, the trusted adviser to my peers who you can entrust with your most complex and important programs at your federal agency."

*—Omowunmi Martins, Student Veteran,*
*University of Rhode Island, Providence, Rhode Island*

Before we start creating *your* personal brand statement, I want to take a moment to acknowledge something that we do in my workshops.

We have a very honest conversation about what's holding us back from communicating our authentic value to others.

In the branding process, and in all marketing message creation, we are taking very intentional steps to guide people's thoughts about us—to think of us in the way that *we want* them to think of us. That is the art of marketing and branding to achieve specific results.

Yet, most of us have heard social programming that hinders our ability to do this.

That programming has perhaps kept you from thinking positively about yourself, your achievements, and your value.

Is it something your parents said? A priest, a nun, a teacher, a professor, a commander, a sergeant, a peer?

Maybe you've even been working professionally with that programming subconsciously in play?

Whatever it looks like for you, it's real. You've been carrying it around. You've internalized it.

And that programming will *not* help you going forward.

This is why we talk about it, acknowledge it, see where it comes from—before we move forward into the branding exercise.

So, what does that programming look like exactly?

## Check Your Baggage

In my workshops with military veterans and military spouses, I ask this question:

"How many of you are reluctant to talk about yourself?"

I'm telling you, just about *every* hand goes up.

You know why?

Because while serving in the military, thinking about ourselves is just *not* a thing we do. We do not get trained to talk about ourselves. In fact, we are stripped of our individual identity - step one as we first put on the uniform.

In the years we serve, we naturally think of ourselves in terms of a unit, part of a battalion, a squadron, a crew, a team. This is our life in uniform. This is how we live and die—through our team, through our crew, through our squadron, all of that.

Then, suddenly, you find yourself in the civilian world, in which you *must* think and talk about yourself as an *individual*.

That's excruciatingly difficult because we've been programmed to think of ourselves as part of the collective—the exact opposite of how humans function as civilians in organizations with pay disparities and structures, where people *compete* intensely to be promoted.

We must be honest about that natural reluctance we feel to communicate our awesomeness.

Here are just some of the reasons vets and milspouses in my workshops cite about *why* they hesitate to communicate about themselves and their achievements:

"I don't want to be perceived as a person who brags about herself."

"What I did in the military wasn't special in any way. It was just my job."

"Who wants to hear stories from this old lady who served in the Navy decades ago?"

"I'm not even sure I want to say anywhere that I am a veteran."

"I find civilians have no idea what I'm saying most of the time, so why bother."

"In my culture, bragging is considered very negative. We just don't talk about ourselves, especially not the women."

Sound familiar?

I give to you this critical lesson because it was given to me: The only person that's going to communicate your value in the way that it should be communicated to influence the people you want to influence is *you*. You might as well get used to it as we prepare to craft YOUR unique personal brand.

How about the other messaging you received while on active duty all those years?

Two years ago, I was at Fairchild Air Force Base, doing an all-day author visit at the elementary school. Afterward, I went to visit my old squadron, the 93rd ARS (aerial refueling squadron). I was touring the new building the squadron had just moved into, accompanied by the new squadron commander. I saw this quote and just *had* to photograph it.

> BE MORE CONCERNED WITH CHARACTER THAN REPUTATION
> CHARACTER IS WHAT YOU ARE,
> REPUTATION IS WHAT PEOPLE THINK YOU ARE.
> - JOHN WOODEN

What a great example of the programming we received as service members!

Be concerned with character. Obviously, that's important—that's your substance, who you really are. *That's* your authenticity.

But this message is telling you to *diminish* what other people think about you. That's the rub and the *contradiction* as you re-enter civilian life.

You *must* overcome that thinking!

To boldly create your new, forward-looking personal branding as a civilian, one trying to attract attention to yourself to secure a job interview or to attract prospective customers as a business owner, you must *undo* that programming!

What others think about you is now *very* important, and you must *craft* what you want that to be! (Sorry, John Wooden.)

In addition to the military training, there may be other reasons holding you back—deep things, real things—things that get revealed in the live workshops and private coaching sessions.

There may be some lessons or messages learned through religious teachings in your background, perhaps something about the meek inheriting the earth or something like that. Maybe there's messaging associated with your cultural upbringing?

As a Latina American, I can tell you that being an assertive woman who boldly communicates her powerful value is not exactly what was encouraged in my conservative home. I was born to Mexican immigrants, and my mom and dad had a very traditional mindset about my role as a girl and as a young woman.

*Calladita te ves más bonita.*

"You're more attractive when you're quiet."

Yeah. Internalize THAT message your entire childhood and see how easily you find your voice—to not only voice an opinion but then to intentionally say something positive about yourself? No. Not happening. I struggled for years with that. I meet *many* other Latinas and Latina veterans doing the same.

I'll never forget the Latina Army veteran I met during my very first workshop in Baltimore. Her transition-induced identity crisis was being made worse by her own mother, who said to her, "Now that you're done playing Army, when are you going to get married?"

Can you imagine enduring *that* cultural baggage on top of all the other chaos during the transition process, plus a full-time schedule as an undergraduate student? She was hurting. She shared this with me, and I was happy to help her shift her mindset so she could look *forward* and communicate her amazing *value*.

All of these are examples of programming we have received up until this point in our lives. This is why we're discussing it: to acknowledge where that hesitation comes from in *your* case, so that we can move *beyond* that limitation.

Remember earlier when I said that branding is a windshield exercise?

It is a *forward*-looking exercise, to create a distinctive message to attract people to you to cause something to happen.

It's literally the opposite of maintaining the status quo, the opposite of all that messaging that's been holding us back.

I have a quote I want to share with you from Sonia Sotomayor's amazing autobiography, *My Beloved World*. On page 218 she says,

> *"Virtue in obscurity is rewarded only in heaven.*
> *To be successful in this life, you must be*
> *known to other people."*

There she is, a Puerto Rican woman from The Bronx, now a Supreme Court Justice. Her story of how she came to understand the importance of her personal brand is instructive to us all.

How did Ms. Sotomayor overcome the cultural traditions I've described earlier, that hold back too many Latinas? How did she instead step into the limelight to promote her achievements?

How did she come to recognize and appreciate her value? How did she learn to communicate it?

How did she become *known* to the people who create lists of potential appointees as federal judges?

And how did she become *known* to the people who make up the short list of SCOTUS nominees so that *her* name could come up when it was time for President Obama to nominate a new Justice to the Supreme Court?

*My Beloved World* is an extraordinary book, and that quote is super special. It's worth repeating it, writing it, even printing and framing it, and internalizing it as a form of motivation to overcome the most powerful resistance we feel.

*"Virtue in obscurity is rewarded only in heaven.*
*To be successful in this life, you must be*
*known to other people."*

In the workshop, after I share her quote, we prepare to ditch that which is holding us back after acknowledging the programming and its origins.

We place our hands in front of our bodies, figuratively holding all that programming in our hands. We tell ourselves that none of it is going to help us going forward. Then we throw that limiting programming behind us over our shoulder.

Go ahead. Do this, if you'd like.

Just pantomime throwing all that unnecessary, limited programming away…behind you…leaving that baggage in the rear-view mirror.

"I'm Denny, aspiring Human Resources professional with a strong background in personnel management, taking initiative, and implementing best practices. I'm a proven operations leader of cultural change in organizations with a keen eye for forecasting and improving efficiencies. Whether leading a group of Army Rangers in Iraq, organizing community stakeholders to improve student veteran outcomes, or cross-pollinating process knowledge across the state's college campuses, I'm the tenacious organizer who exudes initiative, strategic planning, and implementation who you can entrust with your organization's human resources needs."

—*Denny Cosmos, U.S. Army veteran, Student at*
*University of Rhode Island, Providence, Rhode Island*

# It's Not About You, It's About Your Value

Let me share an experience I had at my first civilian workplace after my transition. It's how I came to appreciate the necessity of communicating one's value—something I resisted for years after leaving the Air Force.

My mentor at my first post-military job, Siemens Enterprise Networks in Silicon Valley, was named Yvette Castañon. Yvette was a marketing executive in a sister department, with responsibilities for key parts of U.S. marketing; I reported to the Global Marketing team headquartered in Munich, Germany.

One Friday afternoon, Yvette and I were talking. I was expressing my frustration about how it felt like nobody knew about a massive, global research project I had just coordinated with a marketing firm in Toronto, Canada. I knew that the research findings, and the resultant white paper I had finished writing, would help our sales teams worldwide. With this new research, blended with powerful testimonials I had gathered from our early-adopting customers, our sales teams would be able to sell more solutions sooner and realize more revenue for our business unit.

I asked Yvette something like, "Why don't other managers in global and U.S. marketing know about this ground-breaking work my team and I have been doing?"

Yvette asked me if I had told those managers about the project.

I responded with, "No, I haven't. But doesn't my manager do that? At your management meetings, doesn't she tell you about the most important projects each of us is working on?"

Yvette informed me that, no, that's not at all what happens in departmental marketing management meetings. I was dumbfounded. Looking back, I'm almost certain she was on the verge of laughing at my ignorance, but she didn't.

Coming from a military culture, where good officers make a point to tell their superiors about the excellent work being done by subordinates, including those who have taken on additional duties, I was incredulous to learn that my manager *wasn't* regularly sharing information about my key projects with her executives. In fact, I was learning that nobody, besides my manager and immediate team peers, knew *anything* I was doing.

Worse, Yvette was telling me that it was up to *me* to talk about myself and my work if I wanted others to know. I told her that I did not want to be forced to talk about myself.

Yvette responded with, "Graciela, it's not talking about yourself. You need to learn to think about it as talking about your *value* to the organization."

I remember feeling stunned at that distinction.

If you're reading this, you might have the same resistance to talking about yourself. You might think you should just do your work and the right people will notice, right?

Yeah, I get it. That way would be easiest for you because you wouldn't have to do anything extra—just put your head down, do your work and get noticed, get promoted, and receive a pay raise...right?

Um...no. It's *not* going to happen that way. In the civilian workplace, that's called "wishful thinking."

Yvette broke it to me, "Only *you* will inform others of the work you do and why it matters."

Yvette gave me something specific to do that I'll share with you here. You'll be able to use this communication tactic in your next work environment and save yourself the pain and frustration I felt for years, undervalued and underappreciated.

*This is a very valuable piece of advice.* It's really where I got my first lesson in the power of creating my personal brand: telling an intentional story, to a specific audience, to cause something to happen.

Yvette advised me to take ten minutes every Friday after lunch.

She said, "Write a short email to your manager's peers and her boss. Tell them about your hottest, most important project, and the progress made on it this week. Crucially, *tell them what's in it for THEM.* This is how you will inform them of how valuable you are to several departments."

Yvette talked me through *how* to tell the story I wanted each departmental manager to hear in order to appreciate my work. She taught me how to use the global department calendar to *tailor* my message to each person. In other words, she taught me how to *market* my work output to each person who could benefit from it.

She emphasized the need to do this *weekly* to ensure that all managers around the department would always know what I was doing and why it mattered to *them.* She taught me it was *my* job to be known to other people!

Mind. Blown. Once I got over the shock, I developed a plan.

My boss was a director, so I addressed the email to her six director peers in our global department. I copied my manager. What did I say in that first email? I simply told them the value of my work with the marketing research firm in Toronto. I talked about the project and mentioned I had written a technical white paper summarizing key findings.

For each manager, whose functions and responsibilities I knew about at a basic level, I consulted the marketing calendar of major events. For one executive who worked closely with technical sales, I wrote, "Aren't you hosting a global CIO (Chief Information Officer) Summit in London next month? Why not get a digital copy of the research white paper to each attendee *in advance* of the Summit to showcase our industry thought leadership? And have our global sales team provide a printed copy of the paper at the Summit as they set up one-to-one prospecting meetings?"

For the executive in charge of training global sales teams on our latest marketing initiatives, I added, "Did you know we're currently translating this new research white paper into five languages? You can add this new deliverable to the sales toolbox when you do the sales training in Sao Paolo, Brazil, in April." And so I went... communicating with each and every marketing Director and our Vice President.

Look carefully: I wasn't saying, "Look at me and what I'm doing!"

No, instead, I was communicating, "This is the project I'm working on, and this is how *you* can use the output from my valuable work. This is what's in it for *you*."

Yvette taught me to take a few minutes each week to intentionally share stories about the value of my work to others in my department. In doing so, she taught me that *I alone* was responsible for branding myself in the minds of influential executives, as a thoughtful marketer, a valuable thinker, and a content creator of important deliverables for use across the company, worldwide.

I followed her amazing advice. I positioned myself as a motivated marketing professional who created top-notch content for use by *many* of our employees across the globe, to help grow our business selling our flagship enterprise applications. I did this by spending only ten minutes a week on communicating my personal branding to the leaders of my department.

I hope you understand that I *never* would have done that without Yvette's mentoring and encouragement.

Never would I have thought about taking the time to write about my work as it applied to the marketing and sales objectives of others. She encouraged me to do this, to choose the right words to talk about the value of my work to a specific audience: my boss's peers and her manager. I accepted that my boss was not going to take time out of her day to communicate what everyone in her department was working on. I understood that if anybody was going to know what I was doing and consider me a valuable, promotable team member, it was up to *me* to get it done.

In the months that followed, I wrote this update sometimes weekly, sometimes twice a month. I understood that I was never bragging (something I despise when I witness others doing it); I was authentically communicating the *value* of my work to serve others, something that was very natural for me.

What happened as a result? When the executives in Munich decided to launch an innovative small unit for a new unified communications solution called OpenScape, a unit that would operate as a scrappy startup within the larger corporation, the executive marketing team interviewed only three product marketers for the position of Global Marketing Lead on that new team. I was one of the three selected to interview…because my value was *known* to those executives.

My interview? The marketing executive came into the room and said just one thing: "Write me a unique value proposition convincing us why YOU should be the marketing lead on the OpenScape team. You have 15 minutes. I'll be back." And she left the room.

My one interview question was literally a personal branding exercise—communicate my differentiated value to a specific audience to cause something to happen!

Fifteen minutes later, she returned with the two other executives making the decision. I stood up and read my persuasive, unique value proposition statement to the three marketing leaders—all of whom were fully aware of the value of my work because I had been telling them via those regular emails for almost a year!

They thanked me and asked me to step outside. A few minutes later, they called me back in and told me I had been selected as Marketing Lead for the OpenScape team—a very visible global marketing position I enjoyed for several years after that. The new role exposed me to even more branding and marketing experiences that helped me grow as a global marketing professional.

Like the inspiring Sonia Sotomayor, I had finally given myself permission and learned how to be *known to other people*. And you can, too.

"I'm Alanna, an aspiring mental skills consultant following a career in the Army, where I was a master resilience trainer and a senior intelligence analyst. I'm a critical thinker completing an undergraduate degree in Kinesiology with a minor in Sports Psychology. I am a problem solver and I'm team focused. I coach swimmers with and without special needs. I look forward to participating in research with you and your program to enhance the lives of tactile and adaptive athletes."

—*Alanna, U.S. Army veteran, student at Pacific Lutheran, Seattle, Washington*

NOTE: Alanna created her powerful personal branding at the "AUTHENTIC Personal Branding for Military Veterans" workshop at the Student Veterans of America Pacific Northwest Regional Conference, hosted at the University of Idaho, Moscow, Idaho.

"I'm Carolina, dynamic problem solver, systems thinker and future federal civil servant engaging stakeholders for program evaluation and improvement.

Whether I'm connecting my employer as corporate sponsor with the local VA office to support a community event for homeless veterans in Reno, NV, organizing Thanksgiving dinner at our South Korean outpost with my Army soldiers and Korean augmentees, or creating a formal employee career development track to build capacity within a company, I'm the versatile, detail-oriented team and program leader who always finds creative ways to contribute to my local community while developing and elevating staff members.

I look forward to bringing my resilience, stamina, and negotiation skills, traits that were critical to the eight-year odyssey completing my Ph.D., to your federal agency, foundation or non-profit organization."

—*Dr. M. Carolina González-Prats, U.S. Army veteran*

# Chapter 4

## Building Your Brand Statement

In this section, you will create your authentic personal brand—just like attendees do in my live and virtual workshops. *Every* student takes home a ready-to-use personal brand. You, too, will get it crafted!

Very importantly, you will learn the PROCESS you can use now, in future career transitions, and any time you need to attract a different audience or a different market segment.

We will do an activity where I will have you write down answers to some *very* specific questions.

Channeling successful author and businessman Stephen Covey, let's begin with the end in mind.

As you develop *your* branding, ask yourself these questions:

1. Is it authentic? (Is this really me that I'm talking about?)
2. Is this the best message I can put forward to influence my intended audience?
3. Does your brand cause the other person to look at you and say, "Really? Tell me more!" or "Wow! I'd love your resumé to schedule an interview and learn more about you!"

That's the type of enthusiastic reaction you want to your personal branding. You want to be so interesting, so compelling, so differentiated in your story, that they ask you for *more*.

That's the hook you want to set: "Really? Tell me more!"

## It Takes a Village

Here's a tool I was given during my transition that helped me immensely during job interviews. This tool is going to help you to formulate your brand.

I was given this suggestion and tool by one of the Hubbel Group women in my community of business professionals in Spokane. (That's the group I described earlier who held my hand through the transition process and mentored me to success.)

You'll find this tool particularly helpful if you struggle with finding the right words to describe yourself and your value. It's a technique you will be able to use repeatedly in the years to come.

I was given a piece of paper with a variety of nouns and adjectives. I made about 20 copies and handed them out to my peers in my squadron. I asked them to circle the words they felt applied to me, and then to return the page to my mail slot in the squadron office. It was totally *anonymous*.

I then tabulated the results and came up with a list of words my peers would use to describe me.

I used that tabulated list (and the physical papers my peers had returned to me with circled words) as an *exhibit* during my job interviews.

When I was asked the dreaded interview question: "Can you please describe some of your strengths?" instead of searching my nervous brain for words and examples, I responded by taking out the stack of papers my colleagues had returned to me.

I said, "I'm so happy you asked that question. I recently took the time to ask my peers to list some of my strengths. My peers have described me as follows..."

Then I shared the most common strengths circled by my peers and offered a story of why I believe those words were selected to describe me.

This technique worked *beautifully* during my interviews. The interviewers were always amazed because they realized I cared enough to ask my peers for their insight and feedback to help describe my strengths.

And you know what else that did for me? It *differentiated* me during the interview process because *nobody* else had done that! Who shows up with a list of strengths provided to them by their peers because they surveyed the group?

I give you this tip because it is *so easy* to do, and the payoff is priceless.

In my live workshops, I provide this handout—a list of nouns and adjectives.

Hint: You can certainly use some of these words, if you'd like, when crafting your personal brand—especially for the first question I'll ask in the exercise.

Here's the list of adjectives I hand out at my live workshops. You can copy this list, you can add to this list, or you can come up with your own list.

# Dear Colleague...

| | | |
|---|---|---|
| Tenacious | Collaborative | Knowledgeable |
| Tentative | Connector | Thought leader |
| Courageous | Instigator | Introvert |
| Creative | Ingenious | Extrovert |
| Submissive | Calm | Trustworthy |
| Outgoing | Go-to person | Energetic |
| Apprehensive | Leader | Team-focused |
| Thoughtful | Technical | Introspective |
| Diffuser | Anxious | Expressive |
| Reliable | Sarcastic | Nurturing |
| Listener | Tough | Persuasive |
| Scattered | Distractible | Multitasker |
| Organized | Focused | |

THIS PAGE INTENTIONALLY LEFT BLANK

Now you have a handy bunch of wonderful nouns and adjectives to potentially use in your personal brand when we start the exercise.

Let me mention another way to collect words you may wish to use in your personal branding work: think back to when one of your colleagues sent you a nice email congratulating you, thanking you, or complimenting you for something you provided to her/him.

Here's an email I received from a colleague at Siemens so you can see what I mean—it's a nice message filled with lovely compliments.

## Personal Branding clues: a colleague's complementary email - use *their* words

"Grace, As you know, I'm in the midst of collecting supporting information for all the claims in the value scenarios so the (sales) regions are confident using the claims in our direct marketing campaign. I've spent 60+ hours searching for and reading analyst reports, white papers, presentations and customer case studies. And once again, I find myself uniquely grateful for the **quality, professionalism and "globality"** of your work. Everything you do is **well researched**, with **legitimate attribution** of data sources; and you consistently cite examples, costs and data facts from around the world. **No one comes close to the complete picture of quality you consistently deliver. Your work is consistently clear, credible and global** and I can easily leverage it for discussions with my partners in any region. **You make it easy** to believe our story. You make it easy to use your work in my work. **Your name is my new favorite search keyword in our** global sales/marketing portal. I just wanted you to know once again, I think you are **standard bearer for great marketing deliverables.** Thank you!"
— Tressa Brophy, Director, Installed Base Marketing Programs, Global Marketing and Communications, Siemens Enterprise Networks

What I did here was simply highlight words that *might be useful* to develop my brand.

I'm showing you this so you'll think, "Ah-ha! I have some emails like that, when someone sent me a nice compliment about that one project."

*Please find those emails* and reread the great things said about you and your valuable work.

Highlight the strongest words you feel would influence the types of people you need to attract *next*.

Can you think of other ways you can collect powerful words from others to help you create your personal brand?

Let's look at a few more examples and get to the exercise to create *your* brand.

## Are You Memorable?

Is the introduction you currently use at networking events generic and yawn-worthy or fascinating and memorable?

I'm reminded of these examples from a book written by Peggy Klaus. I attended Peggy's seminar a few years into my corporate marketing career, long before I became as comfortable marketing myself as I had been marketing technology products.

Do you say something boring like:

> *"Hi, I'm Jill. I'm a teacher."*

Or is your introduction memorable, like this example from Peggy's *Brag! The Art of Tooting Your Own Horn Without Blowing It*:

> *"Hi, I'm Jill. I'm a physics professor. I just took on*
> *chairing the department, and now I think I have to*
> *go back and get another degree in psychology…or*
> *maybe even parenting."*

Which of these people sounds more likable? Who is more memorable?

Remember, when you do this correctly, your personal branding will be sticky—another way of saying memorable. It'll be authentically you, with compelling words you will be able to naturally deliver, in a story-like way.

So, are you boring, or are you memorable?

Another example from Peggy that I recall:

*"Hi, I'm Ed. I'm a biochemist."*

Well, that's not at all helpful if you're at a conference with a lot of other biochemists. Plus, it's also boring, and how many people really know what a biochemist does, anyway?

What are you going to say to be *memorable* to somebody who's hiring biochemists, or somebody who's looking for research partners? Maybe you're looking to join a lab at a university?

How about this, as Peggy suggested?

*"I'm Ed. I'm a biochemist. I'm the kid who got a chemistry set for Christmas at age six and never stopped playing with it. Now I do research for one of the world's largest pharmaceutical companies."*

See how much more memorable that second approach is?

It's a story. He positioned himself in my mind as a little kid with the chemistry set and now as a researcher at a major pharmaceutical company. It's a brilliant example. I'm not likely to forget Ed anytime soon!

And, if I'm a hiring official, or looking for a research partner, I'll certainly ask for Ed's resumé because I'm intrigued.

*That* is what I mean by *memorable.*

I offer you one personal branding statement I use to introduce myself, specifically to event organizers and educators:

> *"I'm Graciela, daughter of Mexican immigrants, who arrived at UC Berkeley with an Air Force ROTC scholarship that led to flying for the Air Force. I loved that decade of global adventure so much that I created a publishing company to uniquely share my aviation service story through bilingual children's books. The award-winning literature we create enables me to inspire both school children and adults at educational conferences around the country."*

See, it's unlikely you're going to meet anybody else at any networking event who is going to say THAT.

I just made myself at home in a very unique place in your *mind.* I shared who I am and what I offer.

Here's another example, this one from my friend Chris, an Army veteran. He was in that first personal branding workshop I taught for student veterans at Towson University in Baltimore, Maryland. Here's the branding he came up with by the end of that workshop. (I'm paraphrasing what I remember. It's close and hits the highlights):

*"I'm Chris, student veteran at Towson University and future State Department employee. I'm the bilingual communications guy who found himself on duty one night in Afghanistan, during a sandstorm, patching broken radio antennas with duct tape. I'm a creative problem solver when time is of the essence."*

Wow! Trust me, that was not his first draft. That took some work in the one-on-one session in the latter part of the workshop.

It's a fine example of exactly of what you can create with guidance, as a veteran, even if you might be thinking (as Chris did in the beginning), "But I'm just an Army guy."

## Extracting Product Attributes Exercise

Now, it's your turn.

Grab seven index cards or seven half-sheet pieces of scrap paper. Let's start getting your brand developed.

I like to call this part the "extracting product attributes" exercise because that's what it is in marketing language.

In this exercise, you will brainstorm from different aspects of your life that you *may* choose to use in your branding. You'll decide what's best to use for each situation after you determine your target audience.

I'm going to take you through a series of questions to help you arrive at the right mindset, the right processes to draw out some of the wonderful things about *you* that you may have forgotten. These will be elements of your life and experiences that may well propel you toward your next opportunity.

In this brainstorming activity, I'll take you through a simple process and give you *one minute* to answer each question.

At the end of this, you'll create your unique, authentic, memorable words to make up your new, forward-looking, targeted brand.

Let's begin.

Grab a pen or pencil and your first index card (or scrap piece of paper). Please follow this process so that when you're done answering the questions, you can spread all the index cards or scrap pieces of paper in front of you to see them all at once.)

Grab your smart phone and open the Clock app to stopwatch mode (or use the watch/stopwatch you have on your wrist).

You'll read the question. Think for a few seconds (10 maximum) and then start your timer. This timer piece is critical! **Take *no more than* one minute to answer each question.**

*Please*, give yourself *only* ONE MINUTE to brainstorm answers. I don't want you to overthink this. Let the most important, immediate answers in your heart and mind be the ones you write down.

If you truly blank out and can't think of anything for one of the questions, don't worry about it. Don't beat yourself up, please. You'll have plenty to work with by answering the other questions.

Ready? Here's the first question:

# Question #1: What would you (and others) say are five of your personality pluses?

At the top of the card, please title it: Personality Pluses.

Now, choose adjectives or nouns. Try to brainstorm five words in one minute, in order to have more to work with when we craft your personal brand. (If you only come up with three personality pluses, that's fine!)

Hint: if you are stuck, refer to the list I provided of nouns and adjectives earlier (on page 89). ☺

Start your watch NOW.

60 seconds later: STOP writing and reset your stopwatch to prepare for the second question.

## Question #2: What are the two most *interesting* things you've ever done or that have happened to you?

At the top of the card, please title it: Interesting Things.

Let your imagination go wild. Have you swum with sharks? Ziplined somewhere? Taken a drive/train/airplane somewhere fascinating? Cheated death? Volunteered for something that terrified you?

This doesn't have to be in a professional setting. It could be a recreational activity or travel memory.

One minute. Start your timer now! 60 seconds.

## Question #3: What have you built?

At the top of the card, please title it: I Built…

This question is *wide open*. What exists because you built it (or helped to build it?)

This might be a team project you completed. Or a program you created?

It could be a deck in your backyard or a vegetable garden. It might be a quilt.

Maybe you built a family.

Maybe you started a club of like-minded people?

**What have you built?**

60 seconds. Start your timer…go!

## Question #4: What career success(es) are you most proud of having accomplished?

At the top of the card, please title it: Career Success.

This could be something from a previous job or your current position. The key is that you're *proud* of being a part of or leading it. It's an achievement. If you come up with two successes, that's great, too! This is all brainstorming.

The words *pride* and *accomplished* are important here.

Go! One minute.

## Question #5: What project are you currently working on that best showcases your skills and talent?

At the top of the card, please title it: Skills and Talent Project.

The reason for this question should be obvious. Some part of your personal branding, which you're about to create, should showcase something you're really good at doing and that you're doing *now*.

Notice I said *some part*. What you're doing now is *not* your entire brand going forward. What is the project and what *skills* and *talent* are you using to make it happen?

One minute. Ready? Go.

## Question #6: In what ways are you making a difference in people's lives?

At the top of the card, please title it: Making a Difference.

Notice the open-ended nature of this final question. This could be something you're doing as part of your profession. Maybe it's your weekend volunteer work?

Perhaps some informal mentoring you do for kids in your community? There are many possibilities.

One minute. Go.

Congratulations! You now have a nice list of "product attributes" to draw upon from different aspects of your life experiences, your work experiences, passion projects, and more. You have authentic highlights to draw upon from different facets of who you are as a *human.*

"I'm Nelda, retired Air Force veteran and former Montgomery GI Bill education advisor. While working at the 144th Fighter Wing, my nurturing personality led me to help build a Family Readiness Program and to have a full-time position contracted. I've assisted military members to take advantage of their education benefits and to reach their educational goals. I can't wait to do this at Fresno State!"

—*Nelda, U.S. Air Force veteran, Fresno, California*

*NOTE: Nelda attended the CalVet Women Veterans Employment "AUTHENTIC Personal Branding" workshop in Fresno.*

# CHAPTER 5

## Choosing Who You Want to Attract

"I'm Brandy, a former gas turbine engineer in the Navy who recently graduated with a bachelor's degree in Science and Nursing from National University. I am competent, dependable, and caring—traits I know you're looking for in your next labor and delivery nurse. I look forward to advocating for my patients and inspiring women and moms at your hospital."

—*Brandy, U.S. Navy veteran, San Diego, California.*

NOTE: Brandy attended the CalVet-sponsored "AUTHENTIC Personal Branding Workshop for Women Veterans" at Operation Dress Code, San Diego, California.

Now, before you can decide which elements on your index cards/papers to use in your branding, which words will be the *most* powerful, you must first think about the *audience* you need to influence to start the next chapter of your life.

*Who* needs to hear about you?

Who do you want to *attract* to you with your brand?

For successful branding, identifying your target audience is paramount. There's no effective generic messaging and branding. Your brand *must* be designed very specifically because you want something to happen.

Remember when we talked about positioning in the first section?

You want your branding message to occupy a *specific* position in a *specific* person's mind…or a specific group of people (like recruiters for fintech startups, or recruiters for healthcare administration, or graduate school admissions officers, etc.)

Who is that audience going to be for *you*?

Here's a cautionary tale, an extreme example of what can go *very* wrong when a military veteran starts communicating about his work experience in uniform *without* any marketing messaging training *and* without regard to audience.

This is an *actual* example from a conversation I participated in on LinkedIn:

> *I will never forget the applicant I had many jobs*
> *ago who listed his duties as "Learned how to*
> *maintain my weapon and kill with it."*
> *My first thought: "Oh, an anti-people person!"*
> [ Source: Elliot Echlov comment on post by Adam
> Braatz: https://bit.ly/2FODU1V ]

Yep. THAT can happen, it does happen, when military veterans are left to figure out essential professional development steps on their own…to their detriment.

Without a marketing and branding mindset, veterans may understandably focus only on telling the prospective employer the literal truth about their work, *instead of* on crafting powerful words to positively *influence* and *intrigue* the intended audience. In so doing, they fail to demonstrate their intrinsic value to the audience, who then does NOT ask for their resumé.

Always remember, when you're looking for your next career, that people hire people they *like*. I struggled with this reality as I transitioned—ever focused only on the *task* and *mission* I was paid to do and lead.

Therefore, a veteran opening an introduction with "I maintain my weapon and kill with it" is *not* going to have the desired effect—no matter how awesome you are with your weapon or how many marksmanship ribbons you've earned. Just NO.

I'm going to teach you to creatively couple your valuable military service experience with *other* fascinating parts of your life experiences, so that the way you are known to other people powerfully differentiates you from all other applicants or business owners.

## They Like You, They Like You Not

Let's talk for a minute about what those people you want to attract might be thinking and why it's so important to differentiate yourself in their minds.

Let's talk about what it looks like from the perspective of your target audience—which could be a potential employer, a potential admissions officer, or a potential client if you have a business.

Do you know that the number of people in the USA alive today who have *ever* served in military uniform is a small percentage? Yep. U.S. Census Bureau recorded that active duty personnel and military veterans combined total only 7.3% of the U.S. population.

[Source: U.S. Census Bureau Report Number ACS-43. "Those Who Served: America's Veterans from World War II to the War on Terror," June 02, 2020, by Jonathan Vespa. *https://www.census.gov/library/publications/2020/demo/acs-43.html* ]

Put another way, in a nation of 330 million people, only 1.7 million women are military veterans as are 16.3 million men.

That means that today only *one* percent of American women and less than 13% of American men have served in the armed services. [Source: Figure 3 of Jonathan Vespa's report cited above]

We, military veterans, are a precious asset class with valuable life and work experiences. All of that is true.

But...every year, per both Veteran Affairs and DoD statistics, about 200,000 service members leave the active duty services. That equates to 547 service members returning to civilian life *each day.*

[Source: Veteran Affairs Report titled "The Military to Civilian Transition 2018". *https://benefits.va.gov/TRANSITION/docs/mct-report-2018.pdf* ]

With numbers like that, even in a country as huge as ours, just saying you served in the military isn't unique enough during your job search.

Sadly, too many service members are flat out lied to as they transition out of the active duty service when they're told something along the lines of "You're a veteran. People will be banging down the door to hire you."

I've heard it too many times from despondent veterans who were exhausted from "failing" in their job search for many months... sometimes even years.

This common lie told to service members has led many to believe there is some level of entitlement, that someone somewhere *owes* them a job. That's just *not* how it works in the civilian sector.

To make that point, here's more from that great article I mentioned earlier, the one by Sultan Camp with an awesome, sarcastic title: "Congratulations on Your Military Service. Now Here Are Nine Reasons Why I Won't Hire You."

I send it to servicemembers I mentor and suggest they read it for what NOT to do.

This fantastic piece of writing, from a veteran who is also a recruiter, will give you *strong* insight into the minds of people who interview veterans *every day*.

My favorite highlights from the piece are:

> *"Your Resumé Is Longer Than the CEO of Our Company's (or Shorter Than a Recent College Graduate's). A long resumé doesn't impress me at all. Even worse, a resumé that has neither definition nor clarity is guaranteed to be placed in the trash. I'm probably going to look at it for six seconds, tops."*

Are you understanding the title of the book you're reading now a little better?

The branding, the messaging, the <u>*what*</u> part, MUST be done *BEFORE* you tailor your resumé for a particular opportunity. MUST.

This is *not* optional—assuming you actually want to be invited to an interview!

> *"The reality is that two out of three job seekers will get their next job using social media. What does that mean to you? It translates to lesser-qualified people using technology to their advantage to get hired. They know how to use each of the social networking sites to the maximum extent in their transition action plans. If you think Twitter [or LinkedIn] is of little use to a job seeker or professional, your competition will be happy to land the job you want because they're using it and you aren't."*

This is the *how* part that comes second—HOW you're going to communicate your new forward-looking personal branding to attract a new audience. At this point in human history, it's just *not* optional to poo-poo social media networks because you don't like them. I hear this too many times from student veterans beginning their job searches who have refused to create a LinkedIn account while in school. That means they have likely *not* been networking their way into new industries of interest. They are *not* known to the people who *must* know about them in order to ever have a recruiter or hiring manager ask for their resumé, to consider inviting them to interview.

To their credit, however, they were *right* to delay creating a professional profile until they completed the self-assessment and personal branding work *first*. Now, with this training, their profile will shine and begin to attract the right people.

This timeless Sultan Camp article, more than any other I've read, provides a roundup of common mistakes made during the military-to-civilian transition. It provides insight into some of the obstacles *you* may need to overcome.

I'm using the word *obstacles* because, in sales and marketing circles, we talk about obstacles and *objections* to closing the deal.

What are the objections your potential customer is going to voice as reasons to not buy your stuff?

Or…what obstacles will be placed before you to overcome during the negotiation?

Think of the parallel to those sales objections and obstacles as they will appear before and during your interview process.

What are the reasons that they may *not* offer you an interview?

What are the reasons that they may *not* offer you the job after the interview?

What are the possible objections in the minds of interviewers interviewing veterans?

Here's what I mean. Yes, there are positive news stories about military service members. There are viral stories of military service members coming home from deployments and surprising family members on social media. These stories *humanize* our community. They're lovely and create good feelings about military service members and veterans in the minds of our fellow Americans…including those who work as recruiters and hiring managers in the places we want to work as civilians.

And, let's face it, there are also plenty of stories in the media that portray veterans as somehow damaged. We've all seen news stories about service members suffering from military sexual trauma, often at the hands of fellow veterans. There are stories about veterans suffering with PTSD who became serial murderers after deadly shooting sprees.

A *Foreign Policy Journal* article in 2019 titled "Updated Data: Mass Shooters Still Disproportionately Veterans" opened my eyes to this fact:

> *"35% of U.S. mass shooters (lone, male, 18-59) are veterans, whereas 14.76% of the general population (male, 18-59) are veterans. A mass shooter is 2.37 times more likely to be a veteran than a random person is."*

> *\*The author reviewed the Mother Jones magazine database of U.S. mass shootings, looking specifically at the 97 shootings committed by male shooters ages 18-59. Of those, 34 of them were committed by U.S. military veterans.*

[Source: *https://www.foreignpolicyjournal.com/2019/06/04/updated-data-mass-shooters-still-disproportionately-veterans/* ]

Here's why I mention all of that: Those images of military veterans that millions of Americans have consumed—positive, negative, neutral—all of those things are in the minds of the people that you're attempting to influence with your new personal branding. You have to first remember this is true.

It's part of the work of the marketer (and therefore the job seeker) to understand the mindset of her target audience.

Certainly, if you're applying to a university for a bachelor or graduate school program, you're very likely NOT to be the first military veteran applicant.

If you're applying for work in a community with no military base nearby, chances are that you may be the first military veteran applicant. If you know how to do this messaging and branding work, this fact becomes your *opportunity* – it's your chance to *differentiate* yourself from other applicants.

If you are talking to somebody that you sense has a negative perception about military service members in their mind, just be conscious of that and let your amazing personal branding story *transcend* any stereotypes.

It's a necessary reality of the process of marketing and messaging— to be aware of the psychographic profile (what's already in the mind of the target audience) why is why I'm emphasizing this here before you craft your powerful personal branding.

Those images, stories, and reports do indeed affect positioning about the category that is *military veterans* in people's minds. In some people's minds, it's super positive—they perceive it as a real *asset* to be, and to *hire*, a military veteran.

In other people's minds, especially those with no experience with the military community at all, those minds might feel quite differently. They're not quite sure if they want to hire military veterans because, again, what they've been exposed to is information spewing from the television and stories they read online. Think about that accidental branding that poor guy maintaining his weapon came up with and its negative impact on civilian hiring managers!

Just keep these extremes in mind as you do this branding work, have that consciousness.

Remember, your challenge is to come up with a message that helps you to *effectively* occupy a position in those minds, to paint the image and idea *you* want to paint about yourself. That picture of you may contradict what's already in their minds. Therefore, it will help if your personal branding statement is *so compelling* that it grabs their attention and helps you capture the mindshare you want.

## Let's Get Specific: Who's Your Audience?

Ask yourself: *who* do I want reading about me and calling me? *That's* your audience. You want to avoid attracting others who are not your audience.

If you're about to start a job search, your intended audience may include hiring managers and recruiters for a specific industry, or even at a specific company.

Are you pursuing graduate school? You'll need to attract admissions officer eyeballs to your branding.

Launching a product as a small business owner? Obviously, you want to attract prospective buyers. Who exactly are they? Describe them.

What is it for you? Banking industry? Healthcare industry? Tech industry? Higher education recruiters and hiring managers? Small Business owners?

Whoever it is that you're trying to influence, how are you going to be thought of and remembered as *special* and *different* from other candidates they're interviewing or reading about?

We're going to create your personal branding so that it powerfully communicates and answers:

What is special about *you*?

What is special about your experience/your value/your education/your life experiences?

How are you going to brand yourself in my mind if I'm a hiring manager? A prospective client? The university admissions officer?

Or maybe you're applying for Officer Candidate School?

Perhaps you're applying for graduate school?

In each of these cases, you need to *differentiate* yourself from other candidates.

Think about it. How can you create an eye-catching brand without first understanding what matters to the *intended recipient*? Answer: you cannot.

If you do, you'll be guessing, and chances are you will be wrong.

In that case, your branding message will *not* have the impact you desire because it didn't catch the eye and ear of the people you needed to hear it.

Really think about your intended audience. Ask yourself:

- What do they care about?
- What impresses them?
- What catches their attention?

Honestly, do you know the answers to these questions?

I hope you know, because if you don't know, you must first find out!

Now, on your seventh index card (or scrap piece of paper), please write down that *specific target audience* for whom you are creating this new, forward-looking branding.

"I'm Bobby, a former Recon Marine and scout sniper. Currently I serve as the Veterans' President at my university, where I go to graduate school. I'm an energetic leader with 100 freefall jumps under my belt. Recently, I volunteered in the Paradise Fire relief effort down in Northern California. I look forward to the opportunity to work for your department."

*—Bobby, U.S. Marine Corps veteran,*
*student at Seattle University, Seattle, Washington*

NOTE: Bobby created his powerful personal branding at the "AUTHENTIC Personal Branding for Military Veterans" workshop at the Student Veterans of America Pacific Northwest Regional Conference, hosted at the University of Idaho, Moscow, Idaho.

# Crafting Your Personal Branding Statement

Now, here comes the fun part—creating your unique, memorable, story-like brand!

Spread the six index cards with your product attributes out in front of you so you can see ALL your responses and their titles.

Now, take your card with the target audience and place it *above* all the other six cards. This card, your *audience*, will now drive your decision making about which words to choose to influence *this* audience.

Look at your target audience card. Think of someone you know who is in that group of people you want to attract. Ask yourself: *What do I want to say to stick in that person's mind, to successfully position myself in his or her mind?*

Before you start writing, let me inspire you with *two* more personal branding examples from our fellow veterans: Brandy and Bobby.

Reference Brandy's gas turbine engineer-turned-nurse personal branding statement at the beginning of this chapter: she's not looking backward at the career she's left; she's looking (and branding) *forward*. She knows what matters to *people who hire nurses*, so she puts it in the center of her branding: "competent, dependable, and caring—traits I know you're looking for in your next labor and delivery nurse."

Now, look at Marine veteran and aspiring forest firefighter Bobby's personal branding statement at the end of the previous section. Bobby shows he understands something that matters to those who hire firefighters to battle wildfires, which he wants to do *next*: "an energetic leader with 100 freefall jumps under my belt."

Bobby has selected *one* aspect of his military training to showcase. He directly related it, in his branding, to his next career AND added relevant *volunteer* work to make him a most *outstanding* candidate. Brilliant.

Now, look at your first card of personality traits. Underline or highlight the words you think would most positively impact your target audience. (Now that you're thinking about your target audience, you may think of other words to add to your list. That's okay...Do it!)

Look at the second, third, fourth, fifth, and sixth card, and repeat the process. Think only about your target audience.

What did you write there that is most likely to impress your intended audience?

If something doesn't pop right out at you that will positively influence your audience, can you think of another answer that will? The idea is to have a set of attributes about yourself that, when woven together into a story, will become a branding statement unique to *you*.

Now, remembering the earlier examples from veterans, and reviewing what you just highlighted as you thought about your intended audience, go ahead and write out your first draft of a memorable, unique statement you can use to introduce yourself to your intended audience.

Look at these index cards from workshops I've facilitated. Use these as examples of *structure*.

Some people start by identifying themselves with what they do *now*.

Here, Jared begins by identifying his academic major and university, before launching into a fascinating and memorable story about *why* he does this work and studies *this* subject. Jared's been fascinated by civil engineering since he worked on the railroad as a conductor. He ends by clearly stating his desire to bring his unique talents and experiences to this civil engineering firm.

I'm Jared, a civil engineering student at Portland State University. While working at Union Pacific as a thru-freight conductor, I became fascinated with the feats of civil engineering that made the railroad possible. While serving as a combat advisor in the Middle East, I used my tenacity and creative problem solving skills to teach and mentor foreign soldiers on complex tasks by overcoming linguistic and cultural barriers. I look forward to bringing my skills and experience to your firm on future projects.

Others veterans and military spouses choose to start by immediately stating their aspirations—a *future* career—and perhaps pair it with something interesting to humanize and differentiate themselves.

See the index card that follows.

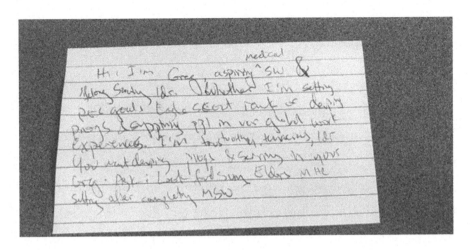

I've transcribed what Greg read aloud at the workshop, from his card, here:

---

"Hi, I'm Greg, aspiring medical social worker and lifelong Scouting leader. Whether I'm setting a personal goal of reaching Eagle Scout rank, developing training programs, or supporting diverse populations in a variety of global work experiences, I'm the trustworthy, tenacious leader you want creating programs and serving in your organization. I look forward to serving elders in your agency after I complete my master's degree in social work."

*—Greg, Student Veteran at*
*Portland State University, Portland, Oregon*

---

Greg wants to first position himself in his audience's mind as an aspiring medical social worker *and* life-long Scouting leader. He adds into his branding his global work experiences, the prestigious Eagle Scout rank, and powerful adjectives leading up to stating his desire to work as a program developer and leader. That's a compelling and unique combination that'll undoubtedly stick in the listener's mind, yes?

However *you* decide to structure your personal branding, make it *yours*. Make it something you can easily, conversationally, communicate.

You'll notice, as you get closer to making it something you really like, that you'll likely think, "Oh, I can use this in my LinkedIn profile," or maybe "This would be perfect in my next cover letter!"

Let's look again at the example from Chris, the student veteran at Towson University.

> *"I'm Chris, student veteran at Towson University and future State Department employee. I'm the bilingual communications guy who found himself on duty one night in Afghanistan, during a sandstorm, patching broken radio antennas with duct tape. I'm a creative problem solver when time is of the essence."*

If you were a recruiter for the U.S. State Department and heard Chris at Townson introduce himself with this fantastic personal branding statement, you might respond with any of these follow-up questions because you're so intrigued:

- Really! Tell me more about your time in Afghanistan.
- Tell me more about that challenging night!
- How did you think of that solution? Had you done anything like that before?

- What do you find attractive about working for the State Department?
- Tell me more about your problem-solving skills when you're under pressure.
- Tell me more about your language skills.

With a compelling personal branding statement like that—targeted, story-like, showcasing multiple key skills and talent—a candidate has differentiated himself from everyone else the recruiter will meet today who does not have their powerful personal brand ready to go.

What story can *you* tell to get those types of questions to flow from your intended audience?

*This is paramount*: you want your audience to remember you, so you must tell them something they haven't heard before. Tell them something so creatively combined, so intriguing, that they say, "Really? Tell me more!"

Tell me a gripping story to position yourself in my mind. Make yourself uniquely *unforgettable*.

Go ahead. Look at what you have captured during the exercise. Write out your first draft of your personal branding statement on a blank index card or here:

_____

_____

_____

_____

_____

_____

_____

_____

_____

_____

_____

_____

Give yourself as much time as you need to come up with something you will use to attract your audience to you.

Feel free to do a creative combination that might showcase your sense of humor. Perhaps you might want to add a little bit of something from your childhood, like Ed the biochemist.

Look at this example—still one of my favorites for how she put this together:

"I'm Martha, a girl raised by a father who taught me about cars and how to build engines. That's probably why it was easy for me to join the Navy and become a sheet metalist…a Rosie-the-Riveter type. Once I got out, I persevered through college for seven years to earn a degree in animal science, useful in my past supervisory positions. I have been characterized as an energetic team builder with a passion for teaching individuals how to become part of a team. I help people to incorporate the company into their lives so that they love their job more. I look forward to becoming your next field supervisor, to continue to grow personally as we grow your business."

—*Martha, U.S. Navy veteran -attended the CalVet Women Veterans Employment Seminar in Fresno, California*

Like the image of Ed the biochemist, this personal branding draws us into Martha's *childhood*. In our minds, we see a young girl fixing engines with her father—she's curious about machines, serving on a Navy ship, in a non-traditional role for a woman, and one she obviously loved.

Of course, you want to learn more and interview her for the field supervisor position! Martha can literally learn *anything* and *lead* your people!

Don't shy away from adding an *element* into your brand that identifies you as a veteran. You likely have at least one thought on one of your cards from your time in a military uniform.

When you have a first draft, step in front of a mirror or turn on your smartphone camera. Record a video of yourself practicing your personal branding. Practice saying it authentically, and in a story-like way.

You'll know when you have it as you want it. It'll sound great, represent the best facets of you to *attract* the audience you seek, and you'll feel GREAT about repeating it to people.

I want to wrap up this section by emphasizing this key point: I have just taught you the branding PROCESS you can repeat, anytime in the future, when you want to update your branding. You can use it when you need to influence a different set of people.

You can review it again in the future when you're making your next career change, seeking a promotion, applying for graduate school, or starting your own business.

In workshops, I often hear this question: "What if I have several different audiences I need to reach? I'm looking for my first job as a civilian AND I'm also starting a business."

Answer: Terrific! I share your ambition and desire to do multiple things at once!

Go back to your cards. Get a new card out and write the second intended target audience on that card.

Look at your answers to the six questions from the lens of this *new* second intended audience. Select the words that will influence *that* audience.

Write a second branding statement to maybe highlight a different accomplishment, personality trait, or achievement to motivate *this* different audience.

Here's an easy way to think about this if you're currently looking for your next career opportunity:

Maybe you're a student veteran graduating next year. You're looking for your first corporate position and first need to impress the 23-year-old HR specialist screener at the job expo table. She's your *first* audience. She's going to talk to dozens of candidates that may all sound too much like each other. You've got this opportunity to brand yourself in a compelling way to be most interesting to her and *not* be forgotten like most candidates she'll talk to that day. (If you've attended job fairs, you know exactly what I'm talking about.)

Assuming you clear that initial hurdle, you will get a chance to meet with some managers or executives during the interview process. You might say slightly different words to them than you did to the HR screener, *building* on the branding that got you noticed!

Write a second branding statement for management/executives, and maybe that version is what you put on your LinkedIn profile. It all depends on who you want to *attract*. Go ahead and experiment!

Feel good that you've learned a repeatable process now. You'll be able to redo this exercise and writing *anytime* you identify a new target audience you need to influence.

That's very important because as you know, the one sure thing is *change*.

# Are You Stuck and Just Staring at Your Index Cards and Scrap Papers?

Let me help you get unstuck and DONE with your Personal Branding!

Yes, I know this is the hard part. This is when most people just sit and stare at their answers on index cards, or just read and reread the examples I have shown.

In fact, during the live workshop, this is the point where I walk around the room and help each student one-on-one. My gift is to see the words you have generated during the exercise, look at your intended audience, and immediately offer up suggestions to begin crafting your compelling, targeted personal branding statement. That's just how my marketing brain works. 😊

Know that I am available to coach you to the finish line!

I just need to see what you've put together during this exercise, and I can coach you privately to get your targeted personal branding DONE and ready to use wherever you need it.

Here's how. Use this link: https://bit.ly/PersonalBrandingAppt to schedule a 60-minute block of time that works for you so we can collaborate in real-time together.

There is a small fee for this private consultation, payable via Venmo @Graciela-Tiscareno-Sato OR via PayPal *grace@gracefullyglobal.com.*

After we've set up your consultation, email your first draft to me at grace@gracefullyglobal.com. If you haven't been inspired with a first draft yet, don't worry. Simply email me a photo of your index cards ahead of our appointment, and I'll have what I need to help you get this DONE.

Let's get you to the finish line…together!

# MODULE 3

## Implementing Your Branding

"I'm Raul Zarate, lifelong technology tinkerer–the go-to-person for family members, fellow students, and faculty members when they get stuck understanding their technology. As a young Marine, I was entrusted to repair electronics, to prepare and maintain aircraft, and other flight-line operations. Today my curiosity as a self-motivated computer engineer has me programming in three different computer languages, and building computers for myself and others. My years as a role model, motivating young people and family members to pursue STEM education and careers, plus my open-minded innovator mindset, make me an outstanding candidate for the _____(internship)."

> —*Raul Zarate, U.S. Marine Corps veteran,*
> *student at Portland State University, Oregon*

# CHAPTER 6

## Testing Your Brand

This part of the marketing guidebook corresponds with the third part of the three-module "AUTHENTIC Personal Branding for Military Veterans" course.

In part one, you learned some basics about the power of branding, its importance, and its elements.

You now know *how* to think about branding and *how* to brainstorm the "product attributes" you may wish to reveal—with you as the "product" that needs to attract an audience and buyers.

In part two, you learned to focus your mind on your target audience, their needs, and what *they* value. YOU did that *ahead of* selecting the words, phrases, and stories from your life to impact and motivate specific types of people you want to attract.

You've gone through the activity to create your own unique, differentiated brand. And, I've taught you how to tailor that brand for specific opportunities, to attract different types of people.

Now I'm going to help you implement and act on this new brand. To keep my promise to a woman veteran that I made years ago, I'm going to teach you how to coordinate and conduct informational interviews. I will help you understand a key concept of networking and why it's important. And I'm going to offer you the opportunity to expand your professional network—through me.

Finally, I'm going to teach you ways you can effectively *communicate* your new brand and show you what the *results* of effective, targeted, authentic personal branding can look like.

## Putting Yourself Out There

Let's begin by putting your personal brand to work with the audience that you want to influence.

It's important to understand, first and foremost, that you have value *now* to other people.

Know how you can prove this to yourself?

Start doing informational interviews.

This will help you to *become known to other people,* and they will, in turn, reveal your intrinsic value to *you.*

This is critically important as you transition, as you may start to have doubts about your value outside the armed forces. I know, I suffered *a lot of doubt* during that phase. I want to do everything to help you *avoid* that ugly feeling.

Remember Julia and her amazing group of women who helped me when I was transitioning from the Air Force to civilian life? Julia taught me a three-step process to use to call on someone I do not know, to introduce myself, and to set up the oh-so-mutually-beneficial Informational Interview. She taught me to talk about the *purpose*, the *process*, and the *payoff* to the person I was calling.

I can't tell you how many times I've made a professional connection for a student veteran I've trained only to be greeted with, "But why would the former Lieutenant Governor of Maryland (or executive/business owner) want to talk to me? I'm just an Army vet."

The simple answer is this: that former Lieutenant Governor of Maryland (or executive/business owner) is a very well-connected business person. He gets frequent phone calls from his business colleagues and friends, asking if he knows people looking for work. Employers are always looking for talent.

So if I've introduced you to my friend, the former Lieutenant Governor of Maryland, and you took the opportunity to conduct an informational interview with him, then the next time he gets that phone call (assuming you've done a wonderful job positioning yourself in his mind!), he'll remember you! He'll drop *your* name to his employer friend, which, of course, makes him even more valuable to *his* network.

Purpose, process, payoff.

We can get you set up with an informational interview to try out your new branding. I'll even provide you with a short script, just like the one I hand out on bookmarks at universities when I facilitate "The Art of the Informational Interview" workshops on college campuses.

I do this professional development training because I realized something after training thousands of college students: you can make it all the way to your junior or senior year in college without anyone ever teaching you *how to* call someone to set up an informational interview, what to actually say, and what to emphasize to make a *total stranger* want to take time from her or his over-scheduled life to chat with you.

The same applies to military veterans and spouses.

That's the model upon which I built the succinct informational interview script I put on the bookmarks I give away. I'll send you the script as a pdf bookmark—just connect with me on LinkedIn.

I also love hearing from people seeking to craft their authentic personal branding and to learn how to set up and conduct informational interviews who are *not yet* on LinkedIn. If that's the case, please email me at *grace@gracefullyglobal.com* and ask for the script on the bookmark, okay?

Then, you'll be 100% ready to call the person I will connect you to: you'll have your powerful new branding, and you'll know *how to* set up an informational interview.

## Learn to Love Networking

Another way to help yourself is to develop lifelong *principled* networking habits. See, doing informational interviews and networking go hand in hand. Principled networking is yet another thing I learned from Julia and her group during my transition into civilian life.

Those ladies in the Hubbel Group taught me to attend events to *give* of myself, something that already came easily to me.

They taught me to attend events with the intention of connecting people I meet that day to other people already in my network.

This is the *opposite* mindset of approaching a networking event as a needy person.

When we first *give* of ourselves, like depositing funds into a financial account, *later*, when we need that network (like when you need your cash), it will be there for you. At that *later* time, we can receive the assistance we need.

That coaching those ladies gave me, about the critical skill set of networking, has propelled me forward *many* times since I left the Air Force.

Since we've touched on the topic of networking with people to create relationships, let me encourage you to intentionally nurture *multiple* networks of diverse types of people. *Do not* trap yourself in a rut with only people just like you—that's the recipe for how to wither away in the sad bubble of an echo chamber.

Here's a graphic I created to share with college students all over the nation.

# Put Your Personal Brand to Work

- Understand that you have value NOW to others
- Start doing informational interviews "to be known"
- Develop life-long, principled networking habits
- Attend to <u>give</u>, not to need and you WILL receive
- Nurture multiple networks – no ruts!!
- "Your network is your net worth"

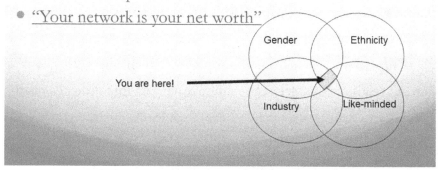

There are many ways people choose to associate. For example, by gender identification, by ethnicity, by their professional industry, by "like-minded" people—which could mean a political affiliation, a religious community, a group of environmental activists, young people interested in learning about personal finance or how to buy real estate investments, etc.

Too often, military veterans *only* associate with other military veterans after they become civilians. I sadly hear this all the time: "Civilians irritate me. I would rather hang out only with other veterans. They get me."

I see this same self-limiting behavior too often in my Latino community networking circles—Latinx professionals who choose to associate only with, or primarily with, other Latinx professionals. I remind them that they, too, are keeping their worlds really small and echoing.

Let me encourage you to kick that default behavior to the curb right now.

There's a fabulous *Forbes* article with *timeless* information that I reference often. It's about how the networks you participate in impact your career performance.

It's titled "The No. 1 Predictor of Career Success According to Network Science," by Michael Simmons (source link is in Resources section.)

What I want to highlight from that *Forbes* article is in this chart.

## The Simple Variable That Explains What Really Causes Career Success 🐦

In December of 2013, I interviewed one of the world's top network scientists, Ron Burt. During it, he shared a chart that completely flipped my understanding of success. Here is a simplified version:

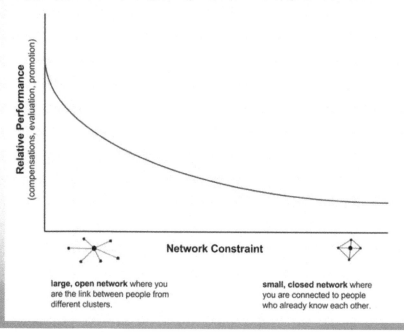

It shows visually what I know to be true after years of working as a professional in several different industries: people who have small, closed networks, in which they're only connected to people who already know each other, have *less* relative performance success, *less* compensation evaluation, and *less* promotion success.

Feel free to read the *Forbes* article for yourself. The key point is right here: The further to the right on the chart you go towards the closed network, the more you repeatedly hear the *same* ideas, which tend to form what you believe. That's your classic echo chamber, ladies and gentlemen.

Conversely, the further you go towards an open network (shown on the left of the chart), where each person is a link between people from different clusters, the more exposed you are to *new* ideas and *new* ways of thinking.

People who behave this way have been shown to be significantly *more successful* than those on the other extreme. This dynamic is *very* important. It can make all the difference in how successful your transition is and how successfully you maneuver professionally in subsequent career transitions.

Here's my advice: please make a point to join *at least* three very different types of groups, with very different types of people. Military veterans should be only one of those three groups.

You should also consider joining a local (or online/LinkedIn group) professional association of people in an industry you're interested in pursuing for your *next* career—you'll discover how wonderful people can be when you intentionally show up to learn from them in order to shape your future career decisions!

My networking circles (and association memberships) include women veterans, women in aviation, Latino entrepreneurs, my local Chamber of Commerce of small business owners, Latino leaders, veteran entrepreneurs, parents raising children with special needs, writers and authors with ties to the military community, student veterans, women who are government contractors, independent publishers, award-winning authors, and more.

I associate professionally with teens in high school, Girl Scouts, college students, young professionals, teachers, business owners, corporate executives in a *wide* variety of industries, professors, retired professionals—*every* age group is part of my professional networking ecosystem.

By having such a broad and diverse network, I can easily give referrals to lots of different people—including *you*—to help them make meaningful connections to move their lives forward. That network makes me a person that is often contacted for referrals to other people, which in turn makes me valuable as a professional contact. I can bring value to many different lives because I *give* of myself this way.

That is what Julia Hubbel called *principled networking.* I absorbed the concept fully into my life.

Similarly, I encourage you to become the hub of *your* networking activity. Make it an intention to *create* these networks around you through time. You want to be right in the middle of different kinds of groups of people. You want to be the person where various, diverse networks intersect, where you know people in several different networks, and you are "known to other people" in several *very* different networks.

As my mentors taught me: "Your network is your net worth."

That is so true. Your network *is* your net worth. You'll see what that means in the coming years as you thrive as a civilian and professional, communicating your value and building and evolving your personal brand.

## Communicating Your Brand

We've spent the majority of this book focused on the process to develop the *content* that makes your brand unique and powerful. That was intentional—the majority of the work the marketer does to communicate about something and motivate people into action is spent doing the hard work of crafting the *message* for the specific intended *audience*.

The *how* part must necessarily come second.

Communicating randomly without doing the work to match message to mind is a recipe for failure.

Want proof? Please see a few of the millions of LinkedIn profiles that were haphazardly put together, without giving thought to *who* would read those words, by people who clearly don't understand the power of differentiated, AUTHENTIC Personal Branding. (Remember the poor guy communicating his skills related to maintaining his weapon and killing people?)

Now let's switch gears to the HOW part.

I'm going to highlight two ways you can immediately put your branding to use, even if you don't already have a website, blog, or social media profile. And, if you do have these digital assets in place, these two suggestions will easily integrate with what you have.

People tend to jump into a social media network and communicate about themselves, hoping the right people will somehow see or hear their content and find them. But, as you've learned, communicating the right information about yourself to *attract* the right people takes intentional effort to get it right.

Please, don't get stuck in the trap of jumping onto yet *another* social network to create yet *another* profile. Be clear on developing your message FIRST and be clear, in our own mind, about WHO your intended audience is that you wish to connect with your message.

Remember earlier, when I showed you my LinkedIn profile ( *https://www.linkedin.com/in/gracielatiscarenosato/* )?

I set that profile up very specifically to catch the attention of educators; I'm on that network for that specific reason, because of my particular business.

And since I initially created my profile there years ago, I have added other products and services to my lines of business, to serve a wider variety of audiences I care about deeply. You can see that I address what I do for each audience in the About section of my profile.

The presence that you'll establish on any particular social media network should also be set up for the *specific* purpose important to you – which includes which audience you want to attract.

The message you'll start putting out there, your personal branding, will first be read by people who already know you and who *also* likely know some of the people who you're attempting to attract.

Because you're obviously seeking to connect to *that* audience, your existing network will begin to introduce you to the people they know and that you want to meet (especially when you ask them directly to do so!) That's how it works. That's how you begin to attract the *new* audience you need to influence if you're not already connected to them.

Here is a promotion tactic to try—*how* you can use your new branding to communicate your value.

There is a wonderful site called About Me (about.me). You can:

- Easily display a short bio
- Link all your social media profiles
- Make the link to your About.me page part of your signature block
- Update this anytime

Imagine your name and just *one* link—clear and easy—at the bottom of each email you send or on your social media profiles. And that one link takes you to your best biography touting your fantastic, memorable new personal branding, with a terrific, brand-enhancing photo.

I recommend About Me as a first solution to test your new branding, *before* you spend the time and effort to create a website or detailed social media profiles. Use About Me to easily *begin* communicating your new personal branding.

"Whether coaching football, mentoring student athletes, or writing a research essay, I am a focused, trustworthy leader. I am the go-to-person who many of the soldiers I helped earn promotions still call for advice. I'm an aspiring attorney with the intention of serving underprivileged communities as a public defender."

*—Charles Howe, U.S. Army veteran, student at UNC-Chapel Hill, on his LinkedIn profile as he applied to Law School*

# A Personal Branding Tactic for Aspiring Public Speakers

Next in the realm of *how* to communicate your new branding, I'll show you a useful deliverable with which you may not be familiar: a speaker sheet.

I frequently make the point that veterans are *very* valuable as public speakers. You may or may not know any veterans who are active on the speaking circuit; trust me—we are out there! There are many of us, speaking on every topic you can imagine.

Let me show you this branding tactic, the speaker sheet, so that if *you* ever have a desire to become a public speaker, you can *easily* follow this template to create your own version of the marketing tool preferred by event organizers.

**Graciela Tiscareño-Sato**

- Air Force Veteran
- Bilingual Keynote Speaker
- Personal Branding Coach & Workshop Facilitator
- Award-winning Author

**Partial Client List**

*CalVet*

*Portland State University*

*Towson University*

*University of Rhode Island*

*University of Idaho*

*Various Public Library Systems*

Gracefully Global Group
22568 Mission Blvd #427
Hayward, CA 94541

Tel: (510) 542-9449

grace@gracefullyglobal.com
www.gracefullyglobal.com

## *Authentic Personal Branding For Military Veterans and Transitioning Service Members*

**In this interactive live workshop AND 3-module online course, military veterans and personnel in transition will:**

➢ Learn what a personal brand is through examples of great personal branding
➢ Identify your most important target audience(s) YOU need to motivate
➢ Learn must-know marketing principles to position yourself as the "must-have" candidate in your job search, college/grad school application, promotion push
➢ Participate in an exercise to craft a compelling personal branding statement
➢ Understand what not to say to a potential employer, admissions counselor, etc
➢ Practice introducing yourself in an authentic, memorable way to showcase your accomplishments without feeling arrogant
➢ Learn valuable communication skills to apply throughout your professional life

In this highly interactive workshop, military veterans, spouses and those in transition will learn key self-marketing skills they will use immediately and throughout future career transitions and professional roles. The presenter, an Air Force veteran with a graduate degree in international business and marketing, will share how she branded herself as the must-have candidate to land a global marketing management role in a European technology corporation upon leaving the active duty Air Force flight deck.

You will be asked specific questions to draw out the most significant, interesting, valuable moments from your military service and life to create your own personal brand to use in the civilian world.

You'll learn how to create several compelling personal branding stories for a variety of situations; you will create at least one you can use with the audience you identify as most important in your life *right now*. You'll practice communicating in a conversational savvy to intrigue your intended audience to ask more about you and your business (if you're pursuing entrepreneurship).

Marketing and networking techniques the presenter used during her own military-to-civilian transition, all workshop content, processes and examples of personal branding created BY military community members are available in Graciela's new 2020 personal branding and marketing guidebook: *B.R.A.N.D. Before Your Resume.*

Now a 10-time award-winning publisher, bestselling author/speaker and professional marketer of technology, events, people and products, she's using her branding savvy to help the military community learn this critical skill set that they'll use and appreciate throughout their professional lives.

This topic is available as a 90-minute in-person workshop, 60-minute virtual group training session followed by individual coaching sessions to cocreate branding, and as NEW 3-module online course. Google "Authentic Personal Branding for Military Veterans course" to find it at GracefullyGlobal.com/commerce.

On the front, you'll see, clearly described, which speaking *topic* I'm promoting in *this* marketing deliverable. You'll see *what* I will speak about, *who* is the intended attendee, and what this audience will *learn* from the experience. You'll also see my contact info, a partial client list, and action shots as a public speaker.

## What People Are Saying

"Graciela is extremely personable and possesses a wealth of knowledge. I wish there were more veterans like her with the skills of public speaking to reach out as she does." - *Kevin Morgan, Student Veteran*

"Graciela blew our students out of the water! Her workshop was very valuable. She engaged us individually, encouraged us to ask many questions and we learned much from her. Graciela's techniques of engaging students were very effective and fun. We left with a clear understanding about how to market ourselves in order to go out into the workforce, start a business or apply to graduate schools." -*Dali Rivera, Student Veteran, Tanann University*

"All attendants were positively impacted--transformed! There were veterans and non-veterans in the audience, and all found the workshop extremely helpful! Not only was the information pertinent to a diverse audience, but it was practical, and sophisticated advice. There were people with criminal backgrounds, substance abuse issues, and severe brain damage in the audience, and you were so compassionate and professional with them. I saw the very clear change in the facial expressions of the attendants at the end of the workshop. They were hopeful, more focused, and connected to their identity as a valuable person and member of the community. Thanks for your commitment to veterans, women, and people of color." - *Joanna M. Arteago La Spina, Community Learning Program Specialist, San Mateo County Libraries*

"Graciela showed us that our skills learned in the military can be repackaged to help showcase our talents. She showed us how to broadcast our skills to others by networking and branding ourselves. Most importantly, she gave us the confidence and knowledge to broadcast our talents to form our own brand." - *Chris Powell, Student Veteran*

Good Night Captain Mama

Buenas Noches Capitán Mamá

Captain Mama's Surprise

La Sorpresa de Capitán Mamá

## Biography

Recognized by the White House as a "Woman Veteran Leader, Champion of Change," Graciela Tiscareño-Sato is a graduate of the U.C. Berkeley where she majored in Environmental Design/Architecture. She completed the Aerospace Studies program as an AFROTC scholarship cadet and graduated with Distinguished Graduate honors. She completed Undergraduate Navigator Training, KC-135R refueling tanker crew and instructor training, and flew with several squadrons at Fairchild AFB in Spokane, Washington. Her first deployment was to Riyadh to enforce the post-Gulf-War NO-FLY Zone in Southern Iraq; flying combat sorties for months earned her crew the prestigious Air Medal, the first Latina USAF aviator to receive this honor.

Graciela became a systems instructor in the classroom and in the jet. She served with NATO Battlestaff in Italy during the Bosnia-Herzegovina conflict, as a bilingual liaison officer at the US embassy in Ecuador and planned and executed a five-nation, 17-day CAPSTONE mission in introducing flag officers to their new posts in Asia. Graciela earned a Master degree in International Management, with emphasis in global marketing, from Whitworth University in Spokane. Upon separation, she was hired as a global technology marketing manager at Siemens Enterprise Networks headquartered in Munich, managing all product branding, marketing and global launches of enterprise applications, serving as media spokeswoman, and presenting to Fortune 1000 executives in two languages.

Now a social entrepreneur, Graciela is the founder of San Francisco area publishing, marketing and communications firm, Gracefully Global Group, LLC. She's the author of several award-winning books including nonfiction *Latinnovating* and her innovative, children's picture books (*Good Night Captain Mama* & *Captain Mama's Surprise*), the first bilingual children's picture book series about women in uniform, inspired by her global aviation service story. She directly serves transitioning military service members, spouses and veterans, the audience for her groundbreaking 2020 personal branding and marketing guidebook titled *B.R.A.N.D. Before Your Resume*. Graciela is a sought-after, intersectional keynote speaker on topics of personal branding, entrepreneurship, innovation, and leadership and also regularly presents in schools. A detailed military bio is available at the Captain Mama site here. Graciela lives in northern California with her husband and three children.

More important content is on the back side; I call it "What people are saying." These are your all-important *testimonials*, where you step back and let other people talk about the value you deliver. Your branding should come through in the words of other people—testimonials are pure marketing *gold*.

When you're starting out as a public speaker, you collect these blurbs by doing a *few* free talks in your local community. Ask every person who invites you to speak for free for a testimonial—no exceptions! You *must* get these testimonials first, from the types of people you want to call you (and pay you!) in the future.

When you put your testimonials on your deliverables, remember to select the best excerpts you've received from the type of people you're trying to *attract*.

In my case for *this* particular speaker sheet, that's testimonials from student veterans, veteran success program managers, and university staff who book professional development speakers to serve their students.

Couple these testimonials with a short biography to round out the speaker sheet. Select the *most relevant* parts of your professional story to influence the people you need to attract to invite you to be a speaker. You'll see what a powerful marketing tool this is.

By the way, you can always find my most updated speaker sheet related to the topic of *this* book by searching "AUTHENTIC Personal Branding for Military Veterans Speaker Sheet pdf." I don't change the template, but I do update it with new testimonials received from happy clients.

I'm hearing in my head right now the question I've been asked many times: "But Graciela...what if I want to speak on a variety of topics to a variety of people?"

Congratulations! So do I! Many speakers are this way because we love to serve people.

The answer is simple: create one speaker sheet for *each* topic, changing the topic description, partial client list, target audience, learning objectives, testimonials (remember those should match the audience who books for *this* topic), and perhaps parts of your bio, to best match up to the topic you're promoting. Maybe you'll want to change up the images as well if you're marketing to an audience for which the imagery on your first speaker sheet is not the best match.

Feel free to look at the variety of topics and speaker sheets I have at the 'Speaking Topics' tab at GracefullyGlobal.com. It's a good demonstration of how a speaker with several topics can create a separate marketing deliverable for each service, with the right personal branding included in each to motivate each audience. *https://www.gracefullyglobal.com/index.php?page=speaking-topics*

## When Branding Works

So, what can happen when you do this personal branding stuff right? What can happen for you when you reach your intended audience, and they call you because you intrigued them?

Well, when you're looking for your next career move, you get asked for your resumé and secure that interview you were seeking—because you were interesting and differentiated yourself.

Perhaps you were introduced to a person inside a company via your informational interviewing and networking efforts? Remember that to get the interview, you first must attract the recruiter's or hiring manager's attention. They may ask for your resumé, which of course, you personalize for their *specific* opportunity.

Let's see other possible results of terrific personal branding.

I can share what I have experienced: the cool things that surprised me once I got my own AUTHENTIC Personal Branding figured out. Here are just *some* of the fascinating moments that happened in my life because I did the work and because, thankfully, the *right* people heard my message.

When people hear your message, they repeat it to others. They begin talking about you and suddenly...a nomination happens. Suddenly, you're getting notified that you've been selected for a regional honor, then a national award for "Entrepreneur of the Year" from *LatinaStyle Magazine*, for example.

Or perhaps your network hears you're writing an innovation leadership book featuring Latino entrepreneurs and business owners—and suddenly, you're invited to launch your first book at the Silicon Valley Latino Leadership Summit held annually at Stanford.

Then you get a phone call from the Congressional Hispanic Caucus Institute in Washington, D.C., saying they'll be honoring all ten of the phenomenal entrepreneurs featured in your book—and you as the author—for spotlighting green economy innovation powered by Latinos.

Or, you're invited to deliver a keynote speech at a large educational conference in Denver—just ahead of President Barack Obama's U.S. Secretary of Education, Mr. Arne Duncan.

Or you find yourself being honored by the White House with nine other women veteran leaders after a nomination process that included hundreds. And then, the next day, your Congressman recognizes you on the Floor of the House of Representatives and enters your story (and personal branding) into the Congressional Record to be forever part of our national archives. *What?!*

Even now, as I reflect and write about these events, which have all happened in the decade since I started my business, in the years I was forced to communicate, market, and brand myself (versus a corporation's tech products), I still can't believe these events occurred in *my* life.

These things happened because someone heard *my* personal branding messages—the messages I *intentionally* crafted over several years, to *attract* certain people to me, in the course of building my business as an entrepreneur, author, speaker, and workshop facilitator.

Through my personal branding, I communicate *authentically* who I am—as a woman, a mother, a veteran, a creative person, an inspirational social entrepreneur—and the work I do through the unique company I created. I demonstrate the *VALUE* of my efforts to those I serve.

Through the years, the message has been received, amplified, and recognized.

It's the most gratifying feeling to know you've learned how to communicate your value, you've been heard, and that you've attracted the people you wanted to bring into your life to make something happen.

This is what I want for *each* and *every* military veteran and military spouse who reads this book, takes the online course, or goes through the branding exercise during my live or virtual coast-to-coast workshops.

I want you to OWN the process of telling the world about YOUR VALUE. I want you to not shy away from it.

I want you to understand that only *you* can best articulate *your value*.

When you do, others will hear it and repeat it. That's *how* you get "known to other people." It's how you *attract* the people you need into your life.

This is true whether you're applying to college straight out of the active duty force, transferring from a community college to a four-year university, or applying to graduate school.

It's true if you're starting a business.

It's true if you're interviewing for your first internship or your first full-time profession as a civilian in the unfamiliar corporate world.

Let me motivate you further to punctuate what I've said several times: the personal branding process you've learned here will serve you for *many* years to come. You'll be able to come back to it for all the upcoming career transitions you will *choose*, and those that will be forced upon you by external forces.

Here's an example from a time, during my *third* career transition post-Air Force, when I used my personal branding to be hired by a start-up company headquartered on the other side of the world.

A solar photovoltaics electronics company headquartered in Israel hired me as their North American Marketing Manager. The role included responsibilities for all marketing strategy, communications, messaging, analyst relations, public relations, and sales support responsibilities necessary to introduce this Israeli technology company to solar installers in the U.S., Mexico, and Canada.

The job opening came to me via a friend, who saw it posted on a job board on LinkedIn. She found the description unique and thought it might be a perfect match for me. It included phrases like "multicultural marketing experience required" and "military veteran preferred" and "mastery of at least one language other than English preferred" a combination of desired requirements you typically do *not* see in job descriptions—few employers would even guess that military veterans have any professional marketing experience.

This company, however, was founded by five gentlemen who, like all adults in Israel, had been required to serve in their nation's armed forces. They, too, were military veterans. They had a strong appreciation for people with a mission-focus mindset. As they started business operations on our continent, they put that desire into the job description for the North American Marketing Manager role, which made its way to me.

You might even say that my professional personal branding message, known to many in my network, *attracted* that startup job opening to me, yes?

During the process, when it became obvious that the General Manager *really* wanted to hire me, he set up my interview with the founder from Tel Aviv, who was tasked with marketing. I asked my future marketing boss this question:

"Why me? I understand you've been trying to fill this position for 18 months. Why are you interested in hiring *me* as your North American Marketing Manager?"

This is a question you can ask, worded slightly differently, during YOUR job interviews:

**Why me?**

**Why are you interested in me as your next**

_____

**(position for which you're interviewing).**

Let THEM tell you the value they see in you!

Even in those times when you do not get hired, you will gain valuable insight as to what wording in your messaging, or on your resumé, was captivating enough to bring you in for the interview. **This is, after all, the one and only purpose of your resumé—to _get the interview._**

That valuable insight will help you in your work to craft and communicate authentic personal branding stories that differentiate you from other applicants.

In my case, I knew the General Manager had already told all five founders about me and wanted to offer me the position. The founder in charge of marketing answered my value question this way.

"We love your combination of global experiences as a military aviator on a crew airplane, which tells us you work well under pressure with others and have a global mindset. Your writing, speaking, and global marketing skill sets are important assets for us, and we appreciate the fact that you're a multicultural professional who speaks multiple languages."

There it is. He demystified which elements of my personal branding, communicated via my cover letter and resumé, were _most_ *valuable to him* as a company founder and executive. That kind of feedback is pure branding gold—so ask for it!

As a business owner, when I get that first call asking me if I'm available to deliver a keynote for an event to an audience of corporate professionals, a professional association, or a community organization, I listen very carefully to what they say about WHY they're calling *me*.

I want to understand which of the many words in my biography, which elements of my intentional personal branding, *attracted* this person to me.

I say: "I'm honored that you're asking me to serve your community this way. May I ask a question? Why are you interested in *me* as your speaker for your event?"

If it's a ghostwriting or marketing or branding coaching client, I'll ask, "Why are you interested in hiring me to do that work for you?"

When you ask these questions, you'll hear different aspects of your messaging being highlighted by different people in different roles, industries, and age groups.

Let *them* tell *you*. ASK the question—market feedback is *critical*. I seek it all the time to know what is working so that I can repeat it and continue receiving new business and referrals.

Here's a tip for entrepreneurs and creative people: When you ask these questions and let prospective clients tell *you* what your *value* is to *them*, they'll have that answer at the forefront of their mind.

Then, when it comes time to submit a proposal or negotiate terms, they'll be thinking of your obvious value since *they just articulated it*! You're more likely to receive the compensation you seek in this situation, versus if you haven't had them bring your value to the forefront of *their* mind.

I'm always asking those questions, and I encourage you to do the same. Make a point to *always* know what people are hearing about your message, what in your personal branding got through to them that motivated them to call. This feedback loop is very important.

What were those memorable, sticky, authentic set of words that actually got through to the people you attracted?

If you ask that question: "Why me? Why are you interested in me?" then you develop the habit of getting somebody else to tell you what your value is—which makes the *ongoing* work of authentic personal branding that much easier!

Remember that intentional, targeted personal branding helps you achieve your desired results.

The opposite is also true: making your message too general, too unfocused, will fail to attract anyone and confuse everyone.

Follow this guidance and put yourself on the pathway to attracting the types of people who will open doors toward the opportunities you seek. This is a skill set you'll use for years and even decades to come as you create new, exciting, still-unwritten chapters of your life as a civilian—where you own your time, your identity, your dreams, and your AUTHENTIC Personal Brand.

"I'm Kristin, Army veteran and domestic violence survivor. I'm a student pursuing a medical records degree and building a loving home for my two boys. I am determined to help empower others to live their best life, achieve their goals and dreams no matter how big or small. I am looking forward to serving your organization as a community partner and as a survivor mentor."

*—Kristin Fox, U.S. Army veteran, student at Columbia Basin Community College, Pasco, Washington*

NOTE: Kristin created her powerful personal branding at the "AUTHENTIC Personal Branding for Military Veterans" workshop at the 2019 Student Veterans of America Pacific Northwest Regional Conference, hosted at the University of Idaho. Since her graduation, she has been hired by the State of Washington and was able to purchase her first home for her and her two sons in the summer of 2020. I'm so very, very proud of Kristin's accomplishments.

"My name is Jessica, former operations specialist in the Navy and student veteran pursuing a bachelor's degree in Criminal Justice at the University of Phoenix. I'm a very creative and resourceful person with an entrepreneurial mind. I look forward to working with and caring for young adults at the Kearney-Mesa Juvenile Detention Center."

—*Jessica, US Navy veteran.*

NOTE: Jessica attended the CalVet-sponsored "AUTHENTIC Personal Branding for Military Veterans" workshop at Operation Dress Code in San Diego, California.

# CHAPTER 7

## Next Steps

Congratulations!

You did it!

You made it through!

You completed all three modules.

## Lessons Learned

Let's review all you've learned.

You now know what branding is.

You've learned the **B.R.A.N.D.** acronym:

**B**ecome

**R**elevant

**A**uthentic

**N**oticeable

**D**ifferentiated

<u>B</u>ecome

<u>R</u>elevant to the audience you need to attract to connect you with the opportunities you seek. You must craft messages that are

<u>A</u>uthentic, not bragging or exaggerating, but you must be willing to be seen, to become intentionally

<u>N</u>oticeable, online, offline, to other people, and your messaging must be

<u>D</u>ifferentiated from others vying for attention in the marketplace.

You now know HOW TO think about branding, how to brainstorm the "product attributes" you may wish to reveal—with you as the "product" that needs to attract an audience and buyers.

You've learned to focus your mind on your target audience, their needs, and what they value ahead of selecting the words, phrases, and stories to impact and motivate specific types of people you want to attract.

You've seen examples and crafted your brand using memorable words to address a specific audience. You've begun feeling comfortable communicating your value by practicing *speaking* your authentic branding.

I've delivered everything I promised you at the beginning.

Now, very importantly, just start: Create *something* using this new personal branding.

Here's one more example from our veteran community to inspire you, one of my favorites I've ever heard read aloud at the end of a workshop!

"My name is Stephen, aspiring attorney with six years of experience practicing barracks law as a young soldier and advocate. Whether I'm building an effective combat team, coding a web page, or transporting military vehicles through hostile environments, my attention to detail and problem-solving skills are tested yet remain un-bested. I look forward to being your next successful law student."

*—Stephen, U.S. Army, student at*
*Portland State University, Portland, Oregon*

## Be Known to Other People and Collect Testimonials of Your Value

I'm going to suggest some actions to take to make things happen for you.

First, after your new, targeted personal branding statement is complete, stand in front of a mirror, and practice your authentic delivery. Get comfortable saying these words. In Justice Sonia Sotomayor's words, remember this is a key step to being "known to other people."

You must practice enough that you get comfortable sharing your value verbally (for the networking events in your future, online or in real life). Remember that when you do this, you are not talking about *yourself*, you're communicating your future *value* to others you hope to serve.

You've created this branding because, before you'll ever get the chance to be of service in another organization, you *must* attract

163

someone's attention to open that door for you. That'll happen via an invitation to submit your targeted resumé for an interview or via a direct introduction from someone in your network, introducing you to someone who is hiring.

Second: You may need variants of your branding as time goes by, to address different audiences you need to attract for different reasons.

Gather more words that express your value, words you've received from others in the form of compliments in an email, or recommendations via LinkedIn.

Ask your colleagues or fellow students to circle words on that page of nouns and adjectives I gave you in this book. Those words have the potential to add a powerful punch to your personal branding.

Take what they've provided to you and create a second version of your branding statement, using the words that represent the value *others* see in you.

I suggest this so you can feel your personal branding can continuously evolve as you learn more, do more, and gain more experiences in which you can demonstrate more and new value.

Third, if you're a small business owner, I suggest you email your top ten customers with this question: "Why do you do business with me/us?"

Alternatively, ask them to provide a testimonial. In the marketing and sales process, it's hard to find a more valuable marketing asset than testimonials from customers. It's your value, elements of your personal brand, being communicated by people *exactly like other*

---

*prospects you wish to attract* to your business. Don't shy away from asking for testimonials!

Let me show you some examples of how we utilize testimonials in our product marketing to inspire all you aspiring entrepreneurs.

At Gracefully Global Group, we're creating the bilingual, award-winning Captain Mama book series, books inspired by my decade of aviation service on the KC-135R refueling tanker plane.

See how we treat testimonials received *from* teachers, who buy our bilingual children's books (and pay for in-person and virtual author visits to their schools), to motivate *other* teachers to call me to serve in their classrooms. Visit CaptainMama.com / Testimonials from K-12 Teachers tab. It's here:

*https://www.captainmama.com/index.php?page=testimonials-from-k-12-teachers*

I've built into our business processes that after *every* event, we collect at least one testimonial. I do this for *every* line of business. We showcase client testimonials on our different websites, each of which addresses a *different* market segment we serve.

See examples of testimonials received for keynote presentations at GracefullyGlobal.com / Testimonials and Clients tab. It's here: *https://www.gracefullyglobal.com/index.php?page=endorsements*

Lastly, here's a showcase of testimonials received from professors, middle school and high school teachers, and high school students for the *Latinnovating* book series I'm creating to showcase positive contributions of entrepreneurial Latino Americans in the USA. *https://www.latinnovating.com/index.php?p=speaking-engagements*

In addition, we feature a key testimonial (or two) on our product pages in our eCommerce store, where people come to shop.

See a sample testimonial from a Navy veteran and military spouse, serving as a Veteran Services Coordinator at a community college, on the product page for the online course I created (that inspired this book) titled ***AUTHENTIC Personal Branding for Military Veterans:*** *https://www.gracefullyglobal.com/commerce/?page_id=644*

If you're an entrepreneur, let these examples motivate YOU to make customer testimonials a *central marketing tenet* for your business. Truly, nothing is more valuable.

Think about it: if you have NOTHING to market your products and services other than the words (or video) of happy customers, you just send those out into the world to attract additional customers!

Trust me, I've done this step FIRST for every book, every digital class, and every service I've ever launched.

I ask a handful of people who preorder and receive the new product or course first, to provide a testimonial.

Then we lead our first marketing deliverables using those first testimonials and update them through time, as we gather more testimonials from clients we've served. It works!

Are you working in a corporate environment? Here's an idea: Take a manager or colleague to lunch and ask, "If someone asked you to describe me, what would you say?"

Ask for this direct feedback from those you currently work with daily. As I did with that list of nouns and adjectives I distributed to my peers during my transition—that insight will help you in a very powerful way as you formulate and communicate your personal brand.

Once you've gathered this additional content, you can again tweak your branding to make it a little better, more powerful, more authentic. You're doing the messaging work *first*, as it must be.

After that, you can choose *where else* you want to appear online with this new, forward-looking branding.

## I'm Here to Coach You and Others Who Need These Skills

If you feel like you need more help with your personal branding or know someone else who needs to learn this professional development skill, consider getting the online class that inspired this book. It includes 1-to-1 coaching with me. We will collaborate to craft your personal brand. To create that course, I took the content I crafted to facilitate live and virtual workshops for transitioning service members, veterans, and military spouses and recorded it in three separate modules.

Students go through the exercises you did in this book to "extract product attributes" and to determine their target audience.

Once you complete the course, we'll schedule the private coaching to complete or refine the personal branding language you drafted on your own, as you did earlier in the book.

My commitment to each client is that you'll have your targeted, differentiated branding DONE at the end of this course and coaching session.

Since you've purchased this book, you can use this exclusive promo code at the Gracefully Global eCommerce site—**BRANDbook20**—to save 20% off the cost the full online course *with coaching session.* You can use it to review what you've learned in this book or gift it to someone you love who needs this professional development skill. Buy the course on our site:

*https://www.gracefullyglobal.com/commerce/?page_id=644*

Or, if you prefer to learn on the Teachable platform, you can find the course there too. Here's the link:

*https://gracefully-global-lessons.teachable.com/p/authentic-personal-branding-for-military-veterans*

## Let's Connect

I would love to know how you succeed with your new branding (the WHAT part we talked about), and then HOW you decide to deploy it!

Please connect with me on LinkedIn by searching for my complete name. Here's the link:

https://www.linkedin.com/in/gracielatiscarenosato/

Please mention that you've read this book and/or taken the online course.

My preference is that you connect with me on LinkedIn. I also love receiving emails from people seeking to craft their authentic personal branding who are *not yet* on LinkedIn. If that's the case, please email me at *grace@gracefullyglobal.com*.

I'm in your network now—so please engage me.

Earlier I offered to expand your network through mine. Tell me who you need to connect with for your first informational interviews to move your life and career forward. All I ask is, when you contact me for that connection, PLEASE be specific with your request. Try your new branding out on *me!* I will make a connection for you. This is what I do, at least once daily on most days.

So, please, let's stay connected and help the next wave of service members—the 250 who left the service yesterday, the 250 who will leave the service today, the 250 who will leave tomorrow, the next day, and so on—learn these powerful skills, expand their networks, and achieve their goals.

I want to hear details of *your* transition process (whether it's your first career transition since hanging up the uniform or if it's the third or fourth career change since then).

I want to share in your networking journey and in the success that I KNOW will be yours. Share your personal branding statements with me via LinkedIn. Tell me how you used this knowledge to pursue and land the next opportunity you were seeking. Or share with me and ASK me to help you connect to that target audience you want to attract.

I really do love hearing what you do with your new branding to position yourself for the next chapter of your life.

I love hearing details of the transformative process we servicemembers go through, as complex as that of a caterpillar to a butterfly, as we become veterans and begin civilian lives and careers.

My goal here writing this book, as it is in all workshops I facilitate, was to help you start to open up from within your cocoon and SHOW YOUR AWESOMENESS to the WORLD!

It's my passion work to turn accomplished veterans into epic storytellers and marketers of *their* tremendous value through AUTHENTIC Personal Branding. That's why I travel the nation to teach this critical professional development skill that took me years to master.

Always remember that *you* have a compelling story to inspire your brand and that only YOU can craft it and make it your own. I can and *will* help you, of course, but your personal branding is *yours*.

When you truly understand and appreciate the power of crafting and communicating YOUR personal brand, when you surround yourself with people who WANT to see you be successful, you will attract the people you need to connect with to cause the next changes in your life to happen.

I can't wait to hear what that's going to be for YOU!

"I'm Louie, an aspiring attorney, a student veteran in business school also engaged in public policy advocacy. I am creative, outgoing, inclusive and humble. I was honorably discharged from the Marines and I spent eight and a half years in prison afterward. I am the Founder of Justice Scholar Society of Change. It helps people reenter society into higher education. My goal is to further help people and end mass incarceration, I look forward to being selected to the Alfie Scholars Program."

*—Louie, U.S. Marine veteran, student at*
*Highline College, Des Moines, Washington*

NOTE: Louie crafted his powerful personal branding at the "AUTHENTIC Personal Branding for Military Veterans" workshop at the 2019 Student Veterans of America Pacific Northwest Regional Conference, hosted at the University of Idaho, Moscow, Idaho.

# Extra Inspiration for Aspiring Entrepreneurs: Roundup of Personal Branding Crafted by/for Business Owners at Workshops for Veterans

"I'm James, founder of DRT, a physical security consulting firm. Whether I'm training groups of people in Close-Quarters Marksmanship or Hand-to-Hand Combat techniques, I approach your personal security measures through the lens of a resilient survivor of multiple surprise attacks in a combat zone. I look forward to training your association (or office) of real-estate agents to improve their personal security and situational awareness while they work alone showing their clients' homes."

*—James Malcolm, SFC (Ret.) U.S. Army, Student Veteran, Portland State, as he positioned himself as Founder of a much-needed security business.*

I'm Martha, owner of Employment Transitional Services. I'm an Army veteran who went through basic training at age 39 and wired commercial buildings while training others to do the same. I currently assist transitioning veterans to obtain sustainable employment. How can we partner with your corporation to assist you in meeting your bottom line?"

*—Martha attended the CalVet Women Veterans*
*Employment Seminar in Fresno, California.*

"I'm Kate, the loyal wolf from Hawk and Wolf Columbia Carriers. I was raised with wolves by my mom in western Oregon. When I came to St. Helens, I started to see this community as a hungry pack of wolves and decided it was my job to feed them. We deliver to everyone from hard workers to the sick in bed. I've cared for these wolves as my own pack for over three years. We look forward to having you join our pack!"

*—Kate, Community Member and business owner*
*of food and product delivery service,*
*who attended the workshops at*
*Portland State University*

# Some Favorite Resources on Personal Branding and Networking

*Career Attraction* article titled "Congratulations on Your Military Service… Now Here Are 9 Reasons Why I Won't Hire You" by Sultan Camp

> *https://www.careerattraction.com/congratulations-on-your-military-service-now-here-are-9-reasons-why-i-wont-hire-you/*

Sultan Camp is a veteran and Orion International Military Recruiter. This is one of the best articles ever written BY a veteran that sums up what so many veterans get wrong.

*The Art of Tooting Your Own Horn Without Blowing It* by Peggy Klaus.

This book helped me immensely in my first two years as a civilian, when I was working in Silicon Valley. As a marketing manager, I was happy to market enterprise telecom products but had no desire to market anything about myself.

Attending Peggy's seminar when I worked in Silicon Valley and reading her book afterward helped me understand that I and *only* I owned this process. I had to learn what I didn't know. I recommend Peggy's book highly for many reasons, including that brilliant title.

*Forbes* article: "The No. 1 Predictor Of Career Success According To Network Science," by Michael Simmons

*[ http://www.forbes.com/sites/michaelsimmons/2015/01/15/this-is-the-1-predictor-of-career-success-according-to-network-science/#6fa0e1e33623 ]*

"I'm Myriam, Founder of the new Haitian Dessert Company.

I'm the Haitian-American woman and recent MBA graduate who is putting her entrepreneurial skills to use bringing the Yummy Fruit Cocktail, inspired by Mom's recipe, to our community's events.

Whether I'm organizing a singing Concert group for a church fundraiser, providing inflight translation service for American Airlines passengers using my trilingual customer service skills, or innovating desserts for family, church, or corporate events, I'm the trustworthy business leader you can count on to put smiles on people's faces. I can't wait to bring my creativity and delicious work products to your next gathering!"

> —*Myriam, Entrepreneurial friend of a*
> *Student Veteran at URI who completed*
> *personal branding training*

# Early Supporters

**We are grateful to our early supporters for
their preorders and other support!**

Kristin Fox

Amanda Huffman

Marissa Rock

Shawn Lewis

Nichole Naprstek

Mary Kate Soliva

David Trenholm

Esmeralda Aharon

Marina Rabinek

Luis Lecanda

Donald Bourne

Adriana Rosales

M. Carolina González-Prats, Ph.D.

Shaun McAndrew

Peter Maranan

Raul Zarate

Junette Caloroso

Portland State University Veteran Resource Center
Jason Shockey, Founder & CEO of mycyberpath.com
Words Unite Bookstore
Aliona Gibson
Lori Norris, founder of Next for Vets and host
of the "Lessons Learned for Vets" podcast

"Your AUTHENTIC personal brand is the differentiated story you intentionally tell to attract specific people to you."

*– Graciela Tiscareño-Sato,*
*Bilingual Keynote Speaker and Author,*
*President, Gracefully Global Group*